QUENCH NOT THE SPIRIT

Edited by Angela Hanley and David Smith MSC

Quench not the Spirit

THEOLOGY AND PROPHECY FOR THE CHURCH
IN THE MODERN WORLD

the columba press

First published in 2005 by
the columba press
55A Spruce Avenue, Stillorgan Industrial Park,
Blackrock, Co Dublin

Cover by Bill Bolger
The cover image is *Helping Hands*, a sculpture in wych elm by Michael
Casey, owned by Mullingar General Hospital and photographed by
Corin Bishop
Origination by The Columba Press
Printed in Ireland by Betaprint, Dublin

ISBN 1 85607 498 6

Table of Contents

Introduction

This book is not a festschrift in the classical understanding of that word, yet it does set out to honour a man who, for decades, has been a *vox clara* in the Catholic Church in Ireland and world-wide. It is usual that a festschrift, or its analogue, is produced to honour a significant birthday or jubilee. This book, however, seeks not to mark a significant event, but to respond to one.

In 2004, after a six-year investigation of his book, *Does Morality Change?* by the Congregation for the Doctrine of the Faith, Seán Fagan SM was the subject of a reprimand by the Irish Episcopal Conference for his book. This reprimand is a stain, not on the reputation of Fr Fagan, who has given a lifetime of dedic-ated service to the church, local and universal, but on a church leadership who would seem to disdain the prophetic voices that seek to keep the church continually renewed so that it can speak the eternal truth of God's love to every new generation in a lang-uage it understands.

An underlying theme throughout Seán Fagan's work has been the enabling of human flourishing. He has pointed out how a legalistic theological methodology and authority has not only inhibited this flourishing but has also, at times, led to the diminution of the person. A fundamental principle of the scrip-tures, as so often mentioned in Seán's work, is the liberation of the individual and of society as a whole. Therefore, a fundamen-tal question to be posed is: how does theology, and particularly moral theology, enhance the flourishing that leads to liberation? Answering this question requires open and honest dialogue. This implies that the expression of different views and beliefs is essential if theology is to impinge on the human spirit. A theological methodology which attempts to curtail or narrowly channel theological reflection is doomed to irrelevancy. A moral theology which does not give due emphasis to human experience can easily lead to an oppressive diminution of the people of God.

In keeping with the prophetic nature of Seán Fagan's work, it was decided that a volume taking the strands of his various interests and weaving them into a coherent whole, would both reflect and give honourable testament to his life's work. With this in mind, diverse authors were invited to contribute on a range of topics, and without exception all those invited, many of whom already had burdensome workloads, responded positively. The delight of so many contributors that such a work was being undertaken was heartening and made the job of editing an easier task.

In a classical festschrift, the subject is not usually a contributor, but remains the silent recipient of the alleluias of his peers. In the opinion of the editors, however, this volume would not be complete without a contribution from Seán Fagan himself. The work chosen, 'Spiritual Abuse' was first published in *Doctrine & Life* (March 2001). We believe that this seminal work deserved the opportunity to engage an audience that may not otherwise have been exposed to its important theological insights.

Both editors were, at different times and in different ways, students of Seán Fagan and this volume represents gratitude on our own behalf and on behalf of the countless thousands who will never have the opportunity to thank him personally for all that he has given to the church; and how he has, as 'pastor to the alienated', shown the face of compassion and inclusivity that is so evident in the gospels, but so often lacking in institutional church structures.

Angela Hanley and David Smith
Editors

CHAPTER ONE

Seán Fagan – pastor to the alienated

Angela Hanley

The theologian, unlike the philosopher, works on history. His 'givens' are neither the natures of things nor their eternal forms, but events ... And events are always tied to time ... This, not the abstraction of the philosopher, is the *real* world. *(M-D Chenu)*

This statement is true only to the extent that the theologian is conscious of the importance of a dynamic relationship between theology and the 'real' world. No adult comes into the world from a sterile environment, fully formed and immune from cultural, social and historical influences. Therefore, the quality of a moral theologian, and the theology he or she does, has a profound impact on the everyday lives of the people in their faith community. The theologian, Johann Metz, stressed the importance of the biography of the theologian for theology. Only if a person lives an integrated life as a theologian, owning one's past, seeking God, thinking and reflecting on the reality of life as it is lived, and does not treat theology as just 'the job I do', will his or her theology be credible and prophetic.

One such contemporary, credible, prophetic theologian is Seán Fagan SM, a moral theologian of international repute. He was born in 1927 and grew up in Mullingar, Co Westmeath, then a provincial town of some 5,000 souls. Despite the grim times in Ireland of the 1930s and 1940s, he led an uneventful life in a loving and secure family until age fifteen when his father's death in a traffic accident, and a period of debilitating illness for his mother, left him, as the eldest of seven children, the father (and sometimes mother) figure to his younger siblings, especially to the two youngest children. This experience had a profound effect on him and influenced his theology as he found himself continually placing the reality of life at the heart of all his later theological reflection and discussion.

Immediately on leaving school, Seán Fagan joined the Marist Fathers in 1945. After a year in Milltown, Dublin, he spent a year in spiritual studies in the south of England and then in 1947 he went to continental Europe and spent eight 'marvellous years' beginning in Rome, living and studying in an international atmosphere. An experience not to be under-estimated at a time when Ireland was intellectually and spiritually as well as geographically insular. J. J. Lee, in his book *Ireland 1912-1985, politics and society* said:

> Irish life abounds, whether in the senior civil service, in university administration, or among academics themselves, with people of high, but narrow intelligence. It is impossible not to wonder how much more of their own potential they might have realised if only they had enjoyed exposure to wider intellectual cultures. (p 615).

According to an interview in *The Sunday Independent* of 16 November, 1975 Fagan possessed 'a sophistication rare in Irish people and probably gained from his many years abroad in various European countries.' In Rome, he met people from all over the world. He loved the international experience and gained a deep appreciation, which was reinforced in his later travels, of the role of culture in the formation of the person in society. This also was to profoundly affect his theology.

Prophetic theologian
'Prophecy' almost inevitably conjures up the misguided notion of clairvoyance or foretelling events. But the theologian as prophet is not engaged in such useless activities. He/she is, in the ancient understanding of prophet, 'a disturber of Israel'. In other words, a prophet is a person who asks the awkward questions of church and of state not just because they are awkward, but because such questions require answers, especially as a response to the 'signs of the times'. The prophet does not just ask the questions, but is also willing to offer some answers. As a

moral theologian, in a pastoral ministry that spans more than fifty years, Seán Fagan produced two important books, in excess of 100 articles, more than 130 book reviews (valuable as minitutorials in theology given his knowledge of comparative literature) and participated in many radio and television broadcasts. Through these media he has asked questions about, and offered answers to, a wide variety of issues that have needed discussion within the Catholic Church.

Though his particular expertise is in the area of sexual morality, Fagan has always considered morality in terms of the whole person in society, a society that has a particular history that must be admitted and owned. His broad knowledge of church history, canon law, philosophy, psychology, languages and more importantly, his knowledge and love of scripture, makes his work more than the sum of its parts. This holistic approach means that such a theologian never falls out of touch with his constituency. Though possessor of a superb intellect, Fagan never sought academic honour or advancement because he believed that his apostolate was to lighten the burdens (man-made or otherwise) of God's people, whether that was guilt, fear, loneliness, rejection, desperation or any of the other myriad miseries that beset people. Love rather than the Law has been his guiding principle.

As a theologian, he makes no claims to originality but, in the words of one reviewer, 'he has used the findings of the best of the theological backroom boys, has shorn them of their jargon, and has made them accessible to the ordinary pastor, catechist and to the man and woman in the pew.' This is Fagan's special gift and he has used it to the fullest in writing and broadcasting. It is especially evident in his books *Has sin changed?* and *Does morality change?* two extremely important books of adult formation on morality.

In these books he set out simply and clearly one of the greatest insights that has informed his theology through the years: the need to 'relativise our false absolutes'. While it might be invidious to attempt to summarise a person's life's work by one phrase, all of Fagan's work, whether lecturing, broadcasting or writing has, in one way or another, been directed towards helping people to 'relativise their false absolutes'. This has not just been directed at lay people, but also at church leadership, because the 'lust for certainty' has led to much damage being caused to the church as people, and the church as institution.

Major works

Any attempt to analyse or assess Seán Fagan's writings would really be nothing more than an attempt to gild the lily, for the clarity of his thought and his crisp prose style mean that everything he has to say is laid out, accessible to all. He is not given to 'padding' his writing by expressing meagre ideas in tortuous prose. Everything he has to say is relevant to his topic; he says it with an economy of words and clarity of expression that makes his books page-turners, something rare in theological publishing. (One could say: 'It does exactly what it says on the tin!')

Has sin changed? grew out of a short article 'No more sin?' written for *Doctrine & Life* in 1976. This article was reprinted without permission in an American publication (although *Doctrine & Life* was acknowledged as the source). Unable to sleep one night, Michael Glazier, publisher of documents of the American Pilgrim Fathers, picked up the magazine and was overwhelmed by 'No more sin?' He tracked down Seán Fagan, and told him he would like to see the article expanded and turned into a book. Fagan's first reaction was 'I am a "hundred yards dash" man. I write articles, I don't think I can write a book.' Thankfully Michael Glazier was able to persuade him otherwise and *Has sin changed?* appeared on the bookshelves in 1977, written in just two months. It was chosen by the Thomas More Society for their book of the month club. In the US it is a talking book for the blind. In 1979 Doubleday of New York brought out a special edition, with a run of 50,000 copies, to celebrate the 25th anniversary of their imprint, Image Books. It sold over 65,000 copies worldwide, unusual for a religious book. It was the first theological book published by Michael Glazier, but his firm soon became one of the foremost publishers of Catholic theology in the English-speaking world.

Has sin changed? created quite a stir in Ireland and elsewhere. This was at a time when morality was seen much more in terms of sin and retribution and of obeying the rules rather than as a freely-chosen responsibility. This was also a time when it seemed that the only real sin in the Catholic Church was sexual sin. *Has sin changed?* was a book that called for a completely new approach to sin using a well thought out adult approach that saw it in the context of life choices and behaviour, rather than the childish, simplistic notion of reward and punishment. It tackled the subject under a number of clear headings:

What happened to sin?
What does the bible say?
Is it allowed?
How far can I go?
How sinful is sex?
My conscience or the law?
Am I really guilty?
Does God punish sin?
God's gift of forgiveness.
Can morality be taught?
Let's rehabilitate sin!

It is difficult to single out any chapter as being central to the book since they follow each other logically, developing the thought that we, as adults, have to take responsibility for our moral growth, forming our consciences accordingly, and not abdicate that responsibility by simply conforming to a pre-ordained set of rules and regulations. As a reviewer in the *Irish Catechist* said: '[this book] deserves to be read in every presbytery and publicised in every pulpit, and the more controversy it engenders in every house, private and even public, the clearer our grasp of the answer it gives to the question it asks.'

Even though in some respects it was a book of a particular era, and geared to the general reader, whether clerical or lay, it has stood the test of time remarkably well and bears re-reading, especially as there seems to be a concerted attempt within the church leadership to return to an inward-looking institution, hidebound by rules that admit no dissension. The church Fagan envisaged in his book as having 'much fewer and far less detailed moral rules than in the past, and will focus more on fundamental principles of moral reasoning, deeper insight into human and Christian values, and a heightened sense of personal responsibility among the faithful,' seems less likely now in 2005 than it did in 1978.

Fagan's second book *Does morality change?* written in just three months, and published in 1997 by Gill & Macmillan, is probably even more important than his first. While it is inevitable that he covers some of the same ground, this book is much broader in its scope and more comprehensive in its treatment of morality. He tackles the subject under headings that need no explanation:

Confused by change
Life is change
What is morality?
Morality and religion
Does nature change?
Conscience today
Moral discernment
Responsible parenthood
Church teaching
New challenges

Again, it would be difficult to pick out a central focus of this book, although perhaps the chapters on conscience and moral discernment are the core chapters from which everything else radiates.

Morality is about choice ... what is the morally right thing to do? ... But conscience is more than just decision ... It calls to something deep within our nature, and leaves us with the conviction that we must obey it if we are to be true to ourselves. In this sense, conscience is more than just intellect and will, knowledge and consent. On this deepest of all levels,

conscience is the core of our being as free persons ... Morally
mature people know their own limitations and weakness,
but are constantly open to new information, new insights,
new values and they want to grow in sensitivity and willingness to do good.[1]

Fagan's willingness to inform people and then trust them with
the results of that information is the striking feature of *Does
morality change?* He is an educator in the fullest meaning of the
word. He leads us out of confusion and misunderstanding, out
of a childish notion of morality, points the way towards an adult
acceptance of responsibility, then stands back and trusts us to
use that knowledge well.

Given that it is on the reading lists of many third-level moral
theology courses around the world, and remains relevant for
any Catholic interested in an adult faith, it is no surprise that
Does morality change? was out of print within three years. (I
heard one story where a lecturer in an adult education course, in
desperation, made twelve photocopies of the entire book because it was out of print – the morality of flouting copyright law
wasn't discussed!) We ought to be particularly grateful to The
Columba Press for publishing the second edition in 2003 – a fit-
ting tribute to Seán Fagan in his Golden Jubilee of Ordination
year. *Does morality change?* could simply have been reprinted as
it was, but true to form, Fagan felt it necessary to modify the text
to include some words on the clerical sexual abuse scandals and
is typically forthright:

The abuse cases have alerted us to the need for a radical examination of the clerical culture that enabled them to occur
and the mindset which prompted the disastrous attempts at
cover-up ... The recent revelations may have rocked the faith
of Catholics, but they can also be the catalyst that will open
the way to true reform. A healthy change for the church
would be to relinquish the triumphalism of the past and discover that God may be closer to us in our humiliation.[2]

Responses

It is hardly surprising that *Does morality change?* was well received critically and reviews were positive. It did not make the same media impact as *Has sin changed?* but that is more for reasons of culture and education than anything else. However, many individuals (locally and worldwide) took the time and trouble to write to the author expressing their feelings. Two representative reactions to *Does morality change?* come from a woman in her late sixties and an Amercian Jesuit priest. The woman says:

> As a 'recovering Catholic' I want to thank you from the heart for your book *Does morality change?* and for the healing it's bringing to me in my late sixties. Thanks to people like yourself ... liberation day has come and mindsets are changing (my own big time). Most of my life has been slavery, keeping rules, etc. All along my heart knew I was just a hypocrite but was led to believe it was a 'sin' to question the church, so I did my 'duty' faithfully and nearly perfectly! My sick body paid the price. I won't go on ... another outburst of anger isn't too far away! Thanks again for your great courage and for bringing us the *truth* that does set us free.

The Jesuit priest says:

> I have read and reread your excellent book. I have recommended it to many friends, although I must admit that when I first came across it two or three years ago I was not inclined to either read it or buy it. My thinking was as follows: written by an Irish theologian, and worse still, one who had lived for many years in Rome; must be all bad, even pre-Trent! But then I saw the dedication to my two favourite moral theologians, Bernard Häring and Richard McCormick ... I then bought it and treasure it. Please continue your great work ... With the death of Richard McCormick and Bernard Häring in recent years we are sadly lacking in truly great moral theologians. You and Charles Curran and very few others remain to guide us in the world of moral theology.

Investigation

There have been many other reactions in similar vein to the above, therefore it is very difficult to understand why *Does morality change?* was reported to the Vatican as a book that ought to be examined for lack of orthodoxy. What is even worse is that the accuser was, and remains, anonymous. The disciplinary procedures of the Congregation for the Doctrine of the Faith are a cause for concern for any thinking Catholic. Perhaps it is enough to say that the Catholic Church, for all its preaching on justice, and the wonderful work of many of its priests and sisters, cannot sign the Declaration of Human Rights of the Council of Europe because of its own investigative / inquisitorial procedures. These procedures are also contrary to the spirit of articles 10 and 11.1 of the UN Universal Declaration on Human Rights in relation to the accused person.

The investigative procedure on *Does morality change?* reportedly dragged on over six years, with added impetus when the book was re-published in 2003. It seems the anonymous accuser was ever alert. The eventual outcome of the inquisition was a rather dilute statement published by the Irish Bishops on their website, the text of which would suggest that they were anything but convinced of the validity of their reprimand of Fagan. This, of course, raises the whole issue of the authority of bishops, successors of the apostles, vis-à-vis the bureaucracy of the Vatican civil service. However, as with the inquisitorial procedures, that is a subject for another day.

A man of vision

Though his books in different ways attracted particular attention, it would be a mistake to define Fagan the theologian by these alone. He is not a man of narrow vision and has written about many aspects of church. Given the limits of space, only a representative selection can be discussed here, which means, unfortunately, that very little of his more spiritual writings can be included. That being said, however, all his writings are imbued with his spirituality – it is not consigned to a separate, private part of his life.

As far back as 1965 in an article on seminary training, he said:

> ... authority should be explained as service, with emphasis on the obligation to consult, to discuss ... This kind of training in the seminary would save many a priest the trouble he makes for himself by treating his parishioners as children.[3]

And again in 1966:

> ... We are grown-ups in the family of God and we must contribute our share by study and consultation, by having the courage even to change our attitudes and outlook, and not to shirk the difficult decisions.[4]

His concern about the ongoing formation of priests and religious remained one of the constant strands in Fagan's writing:

> ... nobody grows alone. We are what our relationships enable us to be. Our uniqueness as individuals will be blurred and distorted unless it is continually shaped by a healthy relationship to others ... Celibacy in today's world is a tremendous challenge to religious ... For a convincing witness to consecrated celibacy, religious need to be mature people, 'happy in their own skin', totally focused and centred on their commitment to Jesus. They need to be clear-headed about the meaning of sexuality, aware of their own intimacy needs and responsible in how they cope with them.[5]

This willingness to speak clearly about the functions and responsibilities of religious life was not found wanting when the scandal of clerical sexual abuse of children broke over the Catholic Church. In 1992, a year before Fr Kevin Hegarty published an article by a Limerick social worker on the impending disaster for the church, (costing him his editorship of *Intercom* magazine)[6] and four years before the Irish Bishops had published their guidelines on clerical sexual abuse, Seán Fagan tackled the subject head on:

> What should be our response to this phenomenon? Very simply: admit, accept, adjust. We must first admit that paedophilia is a reality among priests and religious ... It is a problem of our society at large, and since religious are members

of that society, it is only to be expected that they will reflect their own share of the weaknesses found in the general population. As religious we need to accept this fact, not reject it or rationalise it … The matter is too serious for less than full openness.[7]

Contextualising the righteous anger that many people felt at the large-scale cover up of the sexual abuse scandal, Fagan reminds us:

We need to remember that our Christian faith is not in popes, cardinals or bishops, but in the person of Jesus of Nazareth, who is the incarnation of God's love. God trusts us to be his church in spite of our failures and sins. He trusts us with his Son Jesus (in spite of what we did to him), with his word in scripture, with his sacraments, and indeed with his church (and what have we made of it?). It would be a far healthier church if we could leave the triumphalism behind us. Even if we are reduced in numbers, the Christian community will survive. Like Israel in the Old Testament, the Lord may be closer to us in weakness and humiliation than when the church seemed to triumph in worldly success.[8]

Though clerical child sexual abuse received ample media coverage, another abuse scandal, the sexual abuse of vulnerable nuns by priests and bishops, engendered far less press interest, perhaps because it happens mainly in developing countries. In some quarters that lack of media interest might have been a source of relief, not so for Fagan. As someone who was involved in spiritual and renewal courses for religious sisters since the 1950s, he shows particular empathy:

It is easy to say that weakness and sin are statistically normal, a part of human life. The church is always willing to forgive in God's name … but it needs to be aware of false charity … Given the mindset of abusers and indeed the sub-culture their pattern of behaviour indicates … the perpetrators should be prevented from doing further harm by stripping them of their pedestals of power, their priestly status in the community. To complain about losing the huge amounts of money invested in their formation and training is to forget the gospel, to get our priorities wrong.[9]

It is difficult not to contrast this forthright attitude about the remedies necessary with the attitude of the Vatican to the care-fully researched reports of 1995 and 1998 on the abuse of nuns, which lay without being acted upon until they were leaked to the media in 2001. Following the publicity, the only obvious plan of 'action' seemed to be the compilation of yet another re-port by a small group investigating in just three African coun-tries, despite the fact that abuses have been recorded in at least twenty-three countries worldwide.

We are all church

It would be easy to perceive Seán Fagan as some sort of maverick always at odds with the senior leadership of the church, taking pot-shots whenever the opportunity arises, but this perception would be mistaken. His outspokenness comes not from being an outsider or an attention-seeker, but from being very much an in-sider with a deep understanding of the institution to which he has faithfully committed 60 years of his life, and from a passion-ate, irrevocable commitment to the gospel that underpins it.

The church is both charismatic and institutional … It is a fact of human experience that an institution is naturally conserv-ative (preserving its heritage and tradition), more or less pas-sive (yielding to influences from outside), fearful (lest it lose face, control, power or possessions), anxious and careful (guarding its boundaries). These are quite understandable experiences, but they can blunt the charismatic thrust of the church as a movement of the Spirit, and they need to be criti-cally controlled. The witness of church leaders would be en-hanced if their teaching were presented more humbly, recog-nising that the Spirit speaks to the whole church and not only to office-holders … An objective study of church history is a sobering experience, showing how often the institutional ele-ments hindered or even stifled the Spirit. It is no service to truth to ignore such attitudes and actions.

...church leadership, in prayerful consultation with the rest of the faithful, has the task of discerning the gifts, testing the spirits to see if the new initiatives are from God, but their discernment will be seriously defective unless they have a firm conviction that the charismatic reality of religious life is an essential part of the life and holiness of the church. For their part, religious ... must remain true to their vocation to be spearheads, pioneers, Kingdom-spotters, even when it means being a thorn in the side of those whose charism is to discern and co-ordinate ... We need each other.[10]

Again and again in his writings, when Fagan speaks of church, he is careful to articulate that the church is *all* the people of God, not the tiny percentage of the whole that is the male, hierarchical, clerical church. He wrote of the 1987 International Synod of Bishops on the vocation and mission of the laity in the church:

Perhaps there is an element of Freudian slip in the fact of a synod of bishops discussing the role and mission of the lay person ... As subjects they are excluded in principle, and no amount of 'consultation' can alter this fact ... Consultation is simply not enough. Those consulting decide on the topic, its scope, degree of detail, duration and timing of the consultation, and then filter and summarise the results to fit a pre-decided conclusion. Very little of the original response gets through or is really heard, certainly not the depth of feeling. In this situation many laity are tempted towards cynicism and alienation.[11]

Seán Fagan is wholly aware of the ever-increasing alienation of the People of God from their church. He understands the institutional mind-set that tends to create the alienation. In a book review from 1994 he notes:

A weakness in Vatican documents is that the anonymous authors who provide much of the material are seldom world-class theologians who have published their work and benefited from the public debate so necessary for the refinement of theory and the progress of theology.

In many ways he has increasingly become a pastor to the alienated.

Pastor to the alienated

Reading the 'signs of the times', both for the people and the church leadership, has surely been one of his gifts. Through his work, he continually attempts to inform one and warn the other in the hope that some understanding may be reached. There are many examples from his writing, but perhaps one illustrates the point all too well. In a 1974 article, 'Confession outdated?', he teases out the theological implications of the new rite for penance following Vatican II:

> The real mistake would be to encourage *one* form of penance *at the expense* of the others ... If the church is to be a light to the world, it must be a credible witness to the love of God incarnate in Christ ... If the church is truly catholic, it must be a home where all the members feel at home ... If the church is the sacrament of Christ, it must be the visible sign of his forgiving love; not a sign pointing elsewhere, but an open invitation calling all to a community in which people are reconciled to each other, made friends with each other and with God.[12]

This exhortation of almost thirty years ago had particular relevance for the jubilee year of 2000. When the bishops of Ireland, Scotland and England/Wales put forward the idea of special jubilee reconciliation services with general absolution offered to all-comers as a way of unconditionally welcoming them back to church, the relevant department in the Vatican vetoed the proposal.

Charting the beginnings of alienation

For most observers of matters ecclesiastical, the publication of the encyclical *Humanae Vitae* in 1968 is generally regarded as the watershed of the post-Vatican II church, when it began to lose credibility and authority for a significant number of its faithful members. As a moral theologian, Seán Fagan had more than a passing interest in the provenance and the effects of *Humanae Vitae*. In an article on the 25th anniversary of its promulgation he says:

It is true that morality is not a question of numbers and that a majority is not necessarily right in its thinking and judging, but this ought not to be an excuse for ignoring the continuing non-reception of *Humanae Vitae*. To argue simply in terms of obedience or loyalty is to narrow the discussion and to miss the basic questions of ecclesiology. One seldom hears contraception discussed as a moral question in itself nowadays, because after a few opening statements the argument quickly moves on to authority, obedience, loyalty, and these terms are coloured by one's notion of the church.[13]

Five years later on the 30th anniversary of the same encyclical, Fagan was asked to comment again.

It is no secret that the Catholic Church has a major credibility problem in today's world. This is not simply because of the publicity surrounding the tiny minority of clergy and religious guilty of sex abuse ... People feel that official statements of church teaching are too often out of harmony with Vatican II, out of sympathy with the best insights of contemporary moral theology and out of touch with reality.

... It is difficult to accept that the Holy Spirit would ignore the world gathering of bishops in the Second Vatican Council, pay no attention to the special papal commission set up to study the question, allow thousands of testimonies from committed married Catholics from all over the world to sink into oblivion, and work exclusively through a tiny intransigent group convinced that the church should never change, a group of four clerics who worked in almost total secrecy and who finally got their way by playing on the fears of Pope Paul VI.[14]

The issue of divorce and remarriage in church has again become a live issue for discussion in Ireland with the availability of civil divorce. However, as far back as 1972 Seán Fagan was commenting on the official church position and seeking to find a way to connect with the reality of people's lives:

It is a fact of modern society that even in predominately Catholic countries marriages break down beyond repair … Many theologians are now saying that according to sacred scripture, the 'power of the keys' to bind and loose is not limited to non-consummated marriages, but could be extended to all marriages for the spiritual good of the partners.

… Every year thousands of priests and religious are released from their vows, from solemn promises made to God by mature people who had long years of special training to prepare them for the life they were committing themselves to. It is accepted that the Holy Father can grant such dispensations in virtue of his power as Vicar of Jesus Christ. Many lay people find it hard to understand why the church can exercise mercy in these cases and deny it in the case of married people living in far more intolerable situations who sometimes were not fully aware of what they were letting themselves in for … The problem is far … too serious to be ignored by a church which claims to be a light to the nations.[15]

By 2003, the picture was not much different (except it had become more difficult for priests and religious to be released from their vows) and the insights from 1972 provided Fagan's most recent article on divorce with a solid foundation which says much about the progress of the debate.

The basic reason for the church's difficulties with regard to divorce, remarriage and reception of the sacraments is the fact that there has been a theological vacuum in the whole area of sexuality and marriage. Legislation in this area is based on an outdated theology owing little to the insights of Vatican II … There are not two worlds, one sacred and the other profane. All is under God's saving grace, and the natural and the supernatural, the sacred and the profane existentially are one. Unfortunately, this theological vision finds little place in canon law.[16]

With the decriminalisation of homosexuality, there has been much reported about the lives of gay and lesbian people. Some of the most recent controversy has been the wish of homosexual people to have civil recognition for their relationship. There is also the issue of Catholic homosexuals wishing to express their faith in the context of a loving relationship within the family of the church. In an article of twenty-five years ago responding to a plea for a more Christian attitude to homosexuality, Fagan said:

> Whatever about civil law and secular society, one would expect the Christian community to be more understanding. But to many homosexuals, such understanding is not very obvious ... Moral maturity demands that we free ourselves of inhibiting factors such as fear, ignorance and prejudice in order to make responsible decisions. A first step towards removing them is to acknowledge the facts.
>
> ... All human understanding is historically conditioned, and moral evaluation is no exception. There is a history and indeed a development of morals, a fact not sufficiently allowed for in many traditional statements on moral issues ... Because of their greater pastoral responsibility, church authorities will naturally tend to conserve and preserve, and hence be slow to acknowledge such change. Official statements can therefore be presented in over-simplified form and give rise to confusion and tension. They are an important element in the debate, but are not necessarily the last word.[17]

In advising homosexuals that they did not do their cause much good by 'continual criticism of church authorities for not coming out with detailed "decisions", "regulations" or "permissions" on homosexuality,' there is some sense that Fagan expected that theological and pastoral development would eventually bring a new understanding and acceptance of homosexuality, not as a 'disorder' but as another way of being part of the Body of Christ.

However, by 2003 it was clear that theological development had not kept the momentum it had developed from the time of the Second Vatican Council to 1980:

> The church today, in its concern for justice and respect for

human dignity, warns against the harassment and persecution of homosexuals. But it fails to see the contradiction between this and telling parents and families of homosexuals that their children and relatives have a condition that is 'objectively disordered' and are an offence to the God who created them … This is not divine revelation or a message from the gospel, but a 'teaching' that was culturally conditioned and repeated mechanically through the centuries, without any input from the lived experience of homosexuals themselves, who are the temples of the Holy Spirit and as close to God as the writers of church documents. The teaching of the past came from the top down and does not respond to the complexities of today's world.[18]

Seán Fagan speaks and writes simply and plainly, never equivocating on any issue that requires moral discernment. When asked to contribute a chapter in a book on suicide,[19] he employed his usual skill in dealing with a very difficult, very sensitive subject. As with so many other areas in which Fagan comments, he has a strong sense of the historical development and background of the teaching, and he displays significant understanding of how suicide has been viewed by the church through time.

Theologians or historians may be fascinated by the painstaking moral analysis of our Catholic tradition. It was motivated by concern for the purity of God's law and the effort to help people to understand it and be faithful to it. But we need to realise that there is no word of God in pure unadulterated form, a-temporal and a-historical. God's word comes to us in human words, and every human word from the moment when humans first learned to speak is culturally conditioned, reflecting the experience and culture of the speakers.[20]

Unlike some commentators, understanding the background is not a reason to say that such interpretations should remain static. If, in the words of St Anselm of Canterbury, theology is 'faith seeking understanding' then theology must take account of the lived experience of people.

While the moral principles and the discernment process used in the church's traditional teaching are still valid, we need to be much more humble and tentative in our approach today. Perhaps we did too much lecturing and not enough listening in the past. We need to accept that the phenomenon is far more complex than a simple decision to opt out of problems by taking one's life.

... Essentially, the church is a sign, symbol and sacrament of the whole family of God, perfect and imperfect, saint and sinner, a community whose most telling image is the tiny grain of mustard seed which grows into a mighty tree to give shelter to all the birds of the air, where each can feel at home, loved and cherished, whatever their gifts, their weakness or their needs.[21]

Corrective vision?
More important than the sound sense expressed above is Fagan's obvious compassion for, and understanding of, the complexity of human life. This is not something arrived at after the accumulated wisdom and experience of the years. This is evident in all of his writings in the 40-year span from the 1960s to the early years of the 21st century. In his book, *Corrective Vision* (Sheed & Ward, 1994), the well-known moral theologian, Fr Richard McCormick, explained how he uncritically followed the laws and teachings of the church as a young priest, but how experience taught him that life does not fit neatly into the package of laws and rules, (and anyway some of the rules did not really make sense). So he began to ask questions and this led him to look at church in a more critical way. This was not without its difficulties when at times he felt the weight of official displeasure, but he continued asking and answering important questions until his death in 2000.

Fr Bernard Häring, one of the most outstanding moral theologians of the church, admitted that he had to re-think some of his earlier work. Not because anything he had written was untrue or incorrect, but because he felt that he had been too cautious in not wanting to challenge the ruling class within the church. Häring became quite outspoken in his gentle unassuming way, right up until his last book, *My hope for the church* (Redemptorist Publications 1997), published the year before he died.

It is a striking feature of Fagan's writings that they remain consistent through the years. They are consistent in style, focus and content. There has been no need for 'corrective vision' apart from, perhaps, the lack of inclusive language in the very earliest articles (cultural conditioning!).

Forty years ago Fagan understood clearly that:

theology is a living science, a continuous search, and not a book of ready-made answers. At the risk of oversimplific- ation, it can be said that theology in recent years has experi- enced a rebirth [through Vatican II] as thorough and as dynamic as it underwent in the time of Augustine or Aquinas. From the calm and peaceful attitude of a somewhat static posses- sion of truth, it has moved into a dynamic phase, reaching out into new fields and courageously asking uncomfortable questions.[22]

Conclusion

In 1977, in a special issue of *Doctrine & Life* devoted to evangelis- ation, the then bishop of Ardagh and Clonmacnois, Cahal B. Daly, had an article entitled 'The future of Christianity in Ireland'. In it he says that the 90% of the population attending at church every Sunday presented:

unrivalled opportunities for the transformation of the society by the leaven of the gospel. For churchmen, it is not so much a point of arrival and achievement or of self-congratulation as a point of departure, a challenge, of responsibility … It is up to us to use the opportunity which this gives to bring every intellect into willing and convinced captivity to Christ, so that the truth of Christ may set men free.

What has happened in the intervening quarter century? Maybe there was more than just a little Freudian slip in the unfortunate choice of metaphor: 'captivity' suggests helplessness, a lack of autonomy, being bound by rules and regulations, and being in captivity also means being at the mercy of those in authority.

That men like Seán Fagan, and others active in the Irish church, had already risen to the challenge offered by Vatican II to bring every intellect into 'willing and convinced' conversation (rather than 'captivity') with Christ, and were doing a very good job is obvious. That 'their point of pastoral departure, of challenge, of responsibility' was ably and generously discharged is without question. So what happened? The simple, sad fact is that they were prophets in their own country.

If the church leadership really saw itself as part of the greater people of God and not something apart and above, it would have realised that just as the people needed evangelisation, it too as an institution made up of, and run by, people was just as badly in need of evangelisation. But it did not see itself as such, and while it busily preached on the mote in the eye of the other, it failed to see the log in its own and now seems bewildered at the consequences. It surely needs corrective vision. Where better to look than to the visionary theologians, to men and women of deep faith, intelligence, experience, pastoral sensitivity, who have a deep love of scripture, and who are wholly committed to the church they love despite its grievous sins. Then, instead of punishing them, cherish them, sit at their feet and listen to them. Theologians such as Seán Fagan SM, to name but one.

Do not stifle the Spirit or despise the gift of prophecy with contempt; test everything and hold onto what is good.
(1 Thess 5:19-21)

CHAPTER TWO

A Theology and spirituality for church reformers

Charles E. Curran

Seán Fagan has been an outstanding pastoral moral theologian in the life of the church in Ireland and throughout the English-speaking world. He has taken the insights of contemporary moral theology and applied them to the life of the pilgrim people of God. It is an honour to contribute to this volume in light of the contributions he has made both to theology and to the church.

But we all know the darker side of the picture. The Irish bishops, under pressure from the Vatican, have alleged that there are some errors in his book *Does Morality Change?* thus putting him under a cloud.[1] As with many others, Seán Fagan has had no chance to defend himself before an independent tribunal. For Seán and his many friends this was a cruel blow from the leaders of the church he has served so faithfully in so many different roles over the years. But for those of us 'of a certain age' in the church, the action against Seán Fagan adds just one more dark cloud to a very ominous and threatening sky. We, who were invigorated by Vatican II in the 1960s, have seen the promises and bright future of that time wither away.

Problems in the contemporary Catholic Church
The Catholic Church in the beginning of the new millennium and at the end of the long papacy of John Paul II suffers from a strong authoritarianism and centralisation that seem to go against the Vatican II understanding. This authoritarian centralisation of the church in the Vatican shows itself in many ways in the life of the church today. To be appointed a bishop in the church, a candidate must never have uttered even a word

against an existing papal teaching such as the fact that women cannot be ordained in the church or even the condemnation of artificial contraception for spouses. Only very safe men are chosen as bishops. Centralisation shows itself in many other different ways such as in the demand of the Vatican to decide the smallest matters of liturgical language and customs for individual language groups and countries.

Many theologians throughout the world have been condemned in one way or another. No field in theology has felt this chilling wind from the Vatican more than moral and pastoral theology. The list is long and distinguished – Ambrogio Valsecchi, Stephan Pfürtner, Bernard Häring, Anthony Kosnik, John McNeill, André Guindon, René Simon, Marciano Vidal, and myself. Now Seán Fagan joins the list. In addition, there are many other moral theologians who have suffered at the hands of church authority, or have been investigated, whose cases are not that public.

Moral theology has been a neuralgic area precisely because moral theologians deal with the practical issues that people face in their daily life. As we know, most of these contentious issues in Catholicism today centre on issues of sexuality – contraception, sterilisation, divorce, homosexuality, use of reproductive technologies, etc. These moral theologians are not challenging the core issues of faith but rather the complex specific moral issues that people face in daily life. On the whole, these moral theologians have been dedicated members of the church, striving to be faithful both to the gospel teaching and to the signs and needs of the times.

The tensions felt by Catholic moral and pastoral theologians are also felt by practically all those who are engaged in full-time ministry in the church. I refer to these people as the level of lower middle management in the church. People ministering in the field in all areas often feel torn between the official teaching of the church and the needs of the people to whom they minister. Many such ministers try to avoid the problems and contentious issues as much as they can, but this is not always possible.

But in my opinion, women in the Catholic Church have experienced more problems and frustrations than any other group. The hierarchical church will not even talk about the ordination of women in the church. Even apart from ordination, women lack any true leadership roles in the church. Most of the women graduate students that I have had in theology in the last few decades have had a crisis of faith somewhere along the line. What they experience in life is not what they have come to understand about the church. I can readily understand why some Catholic women have left the Roman Catholic Church, but I admire and support as much as I can those who have remained in the church working for change despite all the problems.

The recent paedophilia scandals throughout the world have reminded us that we are a sinful church. The cries of the poor innocent victims can be heard all over the globe. Priests and ministers took advantage of these most innocent and vulnerable people in order to satisfy their own sexual desires. But in the eyes of many, the behaviour of some bishops in the church was even more unconscionable. They put institutional survival and 'the good name of the church' above the needs of the innocent victims. This issue has made every Catholic mother and father aware of the sinful aspect of the church.

Yes, there are many good things going on in the church today and none of us can ever forget them. But many of us who lived through the changes of Vatican II are quite frustrated today. Very often in the last few years, friends of a similar mentality have often asked me the question: 'Is there any hope for the church?'

Meaning of hope
To address this question, we must first understand the meaning of hope. In Romans 4-8, Paul reminds us that hope is not hope if you see the goal or the object ahead of you. Hope is only hope in the midst of darkness. Hope is hoping against hope like Abraham and Sarah in the hope that God would give them offspring. Hope is not based on what we see at the present time.

Hope believes that God is present and working in our world even when we do not see or feel God's presence. Such is the hope that should characterise the community of the disciples of Jesus.

I have just published a book characterising and criticising the *Moral Theology of Pope John Paul II*.[2] One of my negative criticisms maintains that John Paul II has too triumphalistic a view of the church. The church is holy and without spot, carrying on the mission of the risen Jesus in our world. But the pope fails to recognise that the community of the disciples of Jesus is a pilgrim church, even a sinful church, which, in the thought of Vatican II (*Lumen Gentium*, n 8), is always in need of purification – *ecclesia semper purificanda*.

Ironically, many of us somewhat liberal and somewhat disenchanted Catholics have the same triumphalistic understanding of the church. Maybe this triumphalism comes from our pre-Vatican II genes, but its presence cannot be denied. We, too, expect the church to be holy and without spot. We are unwilling to live with the tensions and problems in the pilgrim church. The very fact that we raise the question about there being any hope for the church seems to indicate a triumphalistic notion of hope that has to see what it is we are hoping for. We are reminded of the true meaning of hope from the witness of our mothers and fathers in the Jewish religion. They did not lose hope after the destruction of the cities of Judah by the Assyrian king, Sennacherib, and did not lose hope after the slaughter of six million Jews in the Holocaust. They are witnesses to all of us that hope is hoping against hope.

Without doubt, hope and the paschal mystery of Jesus – the dying and the rising of Jesus – are central realities in the Christian life. The paschal mystery can be understood in different ways. Lutheran theology and spirituality tend to see the paschal mystery in dialectical and paradoxical terms.[3] There can be no doubt that Luther here is following in the footsteps of the apostle Paul. Paul often appeals to paradox – life in the midst of death, power in the midst of weakness, joy in the midst of sorrow. Catholic theology and spirituality have approached the paschal mystery from what might be called a transformationist and not a paradoxical perspective.[4] Catholic theology, in my judgement to its great credit, has insisted that the divine works in and through the human. Thus, the Catholic tradition sees God's truth in human truth, God's beauty in human beauty, and God's life in human life. But the human never fully expresses the divine and is also wounded and deeply affected by sin. Consequently, there are occasions when paradox is true, but the overriding perspective or motif is that of transformation or conversion of sin into good. At times, God's power is known in human weakness and God's joy in the midst of sorrow, but also human power, truth, beauty, justice, and glory point to the greater power, truth, beauty, justice, and glory of God.

The transformationist motif or perspective rests on an eschatology that recognises God's creative and redemptive presences already in our somewhat sinful world, but its fullness will only come at the end of time. The Christian lives out the tension between the 'now' and the 'not yet'. This is the eschatological tension that characterises the life of the Christian and the life of the church in this world. Thus, we need a theology and spirituality of a pilgrim people and a pilgrim church to live out this inevitable tension. We have hope in the power of God working, but we have to live with the imperfections and even the sinfulness of the present. However, even now there are realities in the life of the church on which we can build to bring about the greater presence of God in our church.

Six bases of a pilgrim approach
This essay will now develop six different bases in the Catholic tradition that help us to live out the tension of 'the now' and 'the not yet' with its realisation that the fullness of the reign of God will only come at the end of time, but here and now there are signs and realities of God's presence in the church that we can use in our attempt to bring greater reform to the church.

1. Mediation. The understanding of the church in the Catholic perspective well illustrates the Catholic insistence on mediation

– the divine is mediated in and through the human. The church is a visible human community with human office holders. What I have called the principle of mediation, others call the sacramental principle[5] or the analogical imagination.[6] The divine comes to us in and through the human. The incarnation well illustrates this reality. God comes to us in and through the humanity of Jesus. In reality, our whole understanding of God manifests the principle of mediation. No one has ever seen God. We take from our human experience the understanding of the best that we know and we apply it to God. Thus, God is known as mother, father, good shepherd, etc. The whole sacramental system illustrates the principle of mediation. The Eucharist is the primary reality in Christian celebration and life. God, the Father, through Christ, and in the Spirit is present to us in and through the eucharistic meal. In human affairs, the celebratory meal is the primary way we bring together family and friends to share food and wine, memories and hopes, joys and sorrows. Likewise, the symbols of water, oil, bread, and wine are the signs of God's coming to us. Catholic moral theology insists on mediation in its acceptance of the theological aspect of natural law. How do we know what God wants us to do? Do we go immediately to God and ask her? No. God has given us our human reason by which we can understand how God wants us to use all that God has given us.

In my judgement, the principle of mediation is a glory of the Catholic tradition that thus recognises the basic goodness and importance of all that God has made. But one also has to accept the limitations of the human. In the church, the Holy Spirit works in and through the human. In some Protestant understandings, the church is primarily an invisible society and the individual is related internally and invisibly to God. Here you avoid the problems and limitations of the human, but you also lose the basic understanding of the goodness and significance of the human and God's working in and through the human. To put up with the limitations and imperfections of the human follows from the importance of the human in the Catholic tradition.

2. *Church as God's way.* The church is not a voluntary society but rather is God's way of being present to us through Jesus and in the Spirit. Many groups to which we belong today are voluntary societies. We join to share with other people who have the same goals, ideals, and interests. A good number of Christians today understand the church as a voluntary society, especially in light of our emphasis on the individual and on freedom. We join a church because we like the minister, the people in the church, the music, and even the architecture of the building. But if we find another church that is more appealing, we join that church.

In the United States, Protestants often see the church as a voluntary society, and this comes through in the language they use about the church. In talking about the church, Protestants will often ask: 'What church are you a member of?' You become a member of the church by your free choice. Catholics, especially those 'of a certain age', normally ask: 'What parish do you belong to'? You don't choose the parish; you belong to it!

Here a distinction is necessary. I think there should be some choice about what particular church community you belong to. But the church itself remains the way in which God comes to us and we go to God. We are members of the Christian community because we believe this is God's plan. The practice of infant baptism in most churches reminds us that we do not choose the church as the way to be present to God. We belong to the church in somewhat the same way we belong to human families. Those who share this understanding of the church are much more committed to the church than if the church were just another voluntary association.

3. *Church universal and particular.* The tension between the church universal and the church particular or between unity and diversity exists in the church. The church catholic by its very language is a universal church – a church that strives to embrace all people of all races and nationalities. Here the church takes seriously the biblical injunction of Jesus to preach the good news to all humankind. The church catholic is not a congregational or

national church but a universal church. The danger of a congregational or even national church is identifying God with the goals
and understanding of a particular congregation or nation. The
church must transcend all congregations and all nations in order
to be able to criticise them in the name of the gospel. But inevitably great tensions will arise between the church universal
and the church national or local. Look at the experience of the
worldwide Anglican community today as it deals with the issue
of homosexuality. In a sense, it is much easier to have a smaller
homogeneous church with like-minded people in it, but this is
not the church catholic.

A one-sided commitment to single issues works against the
unity of the universal church. If one insists only on a particular
single issue (no matter from the left or the right) the danger exists
of fracturing the church universal. I can understand how at times
individuals might feel the need to abandon the church because of
a single issue (ordination of women, homosexuality). But as a
church universal, we at times need to be willing to put up with
sharp disagreements on what we think is an important single
issue. Long ago, Paul reminded the early Corinthian Christian
community that there was nothing wrong with eating meat sacri-
ficed to idols. But if a sister or brother in the community were
scandalised by it, he would not eat the meat (1 Cor 10:23-33).

Similar to the tension between the church universal and the
church particular is the tension between unity and diversity in
the church. Without doubt, the Roman Catholic church has
definitely given more importance to the universal church and to
unity rather than diversity in the church. But even here the
Catholic tradition has recognised the need to distinguish the
various levels of church teachings, because all are not of the
same importance and centrality. Some truths are core and central to our faith, but others are more remote and peripheral. Even
pre-Vatican II Catholic theology recognised this reality. Various
teachings of the church were given a 'theological note' which attempted to distinguish how central and important the teaching
was. The highest category was divine and revealed faith and

then went down in less importance and centrality to divine
faith, proximate to faith, Catholic teaching, common teaching,
more probable, less probable, and all the way down to the last
category of 'offensive to pious ears'. Thus, even the pre-Vatican
II church distinguished what were core from what were more
remote and peripheral aspects of faith.[7] Ever since the nineteenth century, Catholic theology also sharply distinguished between infallible and non-infallible teachings. The vast majority
of church teachings fit into the non-infallible category. Volumes
have been written on this subject, but it is sufficient to recall that
non-infallible really means fallible.

Thus, the Roman Catholic Church recognises the distinction
between what is core to faith and what is less central and less
important. Such a distinction does not entail a cafeteria
Catholicism according to which one picks and chooses whatever
one likes. To be Catholic, one must recognise and accept the core
claims of faith: creation, redemption, sanctification, the Trinity,
the sacramental system, and the articles of the Creed. But there
are many other areas, especially specific moral issues, that are
not that core and central to Catholic faith. Dissenting theologians such as Seán Fagan, myself, and a whole multitude of
others have insisted that dissent or disagreement can be acceptable when the reasons behind non-infallible moral teachings are
not convincing.

There can be no doubt that in the present Roman Catholic
Church there continues to be a strong emphasis on the church
universal and the unity of the church without giving enough
importance to the local church or legitimate diversity in the
church.[8] But there are elements in the Catholic tradition that call
for a greater emphasis on particularity (e.g. the inculturation of
faith, the collegiality of all bishops in the church) and the recognition of legitimate diversity in the church as expressed in the
theological justification of some faithful dissent in the church.

The guiding principle in these tensions comes from the old
axiom – in necessary things, unity; in doubtful things, freedom;
in all things, charity. This axiom has been variously attributed to

many including Augustine and Philip Melanchton, but the real author was Rupert Meldenius, a comparatively unknown seventeenth century Lutheran theologian.[9]

4. *The pilgrim church.* The pre-Vatican II Catholic Church was too triumphalistic. The church was identified with the kingdom of God and was a perfect society. The church was holy and without spot. Vatican II rightly criticised the triumphalism in the church. The church is not the kingdom of God but only a sign of the kingdom. The kingdom of God will never be fully present in this world. The church is a pilgrim church that, in accord with the well-known Protestant axiom, is a church always in need of reform and change.[10] Here we see the eschatological tension that colours all human existence between the two comings of Jesus. Just as none of us as individual Christians ever lives the fullness of the gospel, so too the pilgrim church by its very nature always falls short and is, in a very true sense, a sinful church. The church is called to be one, holy, Catholic, and apostolic, but it never fully lives up to this call. Often a poor understanding of mediation has made us forget the pilgrim nature of the church. Yes, the church does mediate the divine to us, but it mediates the divine in and through its human and pilgrim existence so that one cannot fully identify the church with the divine or the fullness of the reign of God.

To his credit, John Paul II has apologised more than any other previous pope for the sins of members of the church.[11] But note that his apologies are for the sins of members of the church and not for the sins of the church. He is not able to recognise that the church itself is sinful.[12] But if the church is the pilgrim people of God, then it will always be a sinful church which never fully lives up to its calling. But, as pointed out earlier, many liberals in the church today also have difficulty accepting the pilgrim and sinful nature of the church. The church will never be perfect. We must constantly strive to reform the church as well as ourselves. Such is the nature of life in the church that recognises the tension between 'the now' and 'the not yet' aspect of the reign of God.

5. *Tradition and reason.* The Catholic church recognises the role of ongoing tradition as well as an important role for human reason. The Catholic tradition has never accepted the axiom of the 'scripture alone'. In keeping with its 'both-and' approach, the Catholic tradition has insisted on both scripture and tradition. A pre-Vatican II Catholicism put these two together poorly by often understanding scripture and tradition as two quite different sources of revealed truth. Now we see the two as very closely related. The scriptures themselves are historically and culturally conditioned. One cannot go from a particular scripture quote (for example, the role of women in church) to a conclusion that is necessarily valid today. We believe that the Holy Spirit helps the church to understand, live, and appropriate the word and work of Jesus in light of the ongoing circumstances of time and place. Tradition, in the words of Jaroslav Pelikan, is not the dead faith of the living but the living faith of the dead.[13] Especially in the pre-Vatican II church there was a tendency to think that tradition stopped fifty years before we were born.

Ongoing tradition has played a very significant role in the historical development of Roman Catholicism. The Christological and Trinitarian councils of the early church well illustrate this reality. We came to proclaim that there are three persons in one God and two natures in Jesus. But 'person' and 'nature' are technical Greek terms that are not found in scripture. The first disciples of Jesus would not understand what was meant by talking about three persons in God and two natures in Jesus. But the early church found it necessary to use these Greek technical terms to understand more appropriately the biblical message about both God and Jesus. It was not enough simply to repeat what the scripture said. The role of ongoing tradition is even much greater with regard to the sacramental life of the church. For the greater part of its existence, the Catholic Church did not recognise the existence of seven sacraments. Only in the twelfth century did we finally accept marriage as the seventh sacrament.[14]

In addition, the Catholic tradition gives a significant role to human reason. Here again, the Catholic 'and' insists on both faith and reason.[15] A famous Catholic axiom recognises that faith and reason can never contradict one another. This does not mean that reason can prove faith, but Catholicism has consistently emphasised that faith seeks understanding and understanding seeks faith. In fact, this describes very well the role of theology. To its great credit, the Catholic Church was the home of the first universities in the West because of its high regard for human reason. Catholic moral theology has given reason a very important role. By using the human reason God has given us, we can reflect on what God has made and determine what should be done. A church that accepts ongoing tradition and a significant role for human reason has the tools to deal with proper development and change in the church.

6. *Church structure.* A sixth basis concerns structures and structural change in the church. Catholics recognise there are certain structural elements that belong to the very nature of the church, such as the office and role of bishops and of the Bishop of Rome. But in the course of history, there have been significant developments and changes of structure within the church. The Bishop of Rome has obviously needed assistance and help in carrying out his role. But the institution of the Roman curia, as we know it today, has changed greatly over time. Only in 1588 did Pope Sixtus V bring about the formal organisation of the Roman curia. Subsequent popes have often changed the structure of the curia with the latest change made by Pope John Paul II in 1988.[16]

The pre-Vatican II church was more authoritative, defensive, and centralised than at any other time in its history. In the role of moral theology, for example, where both Seán Fagan and I work, the pope and the Roman curia began playing a much greater role in the nineteenth century. The curia often intervened to give solutions to complex issues such as the distinction between direct and indirect abortion.[17] Thomas Bouquillon, the professor of moral theology at the Catholic University of America at the end of the nineteenth century, criticised moral theologians

for too quickly looking for answers from the Roman Congregations.[18]

Vatican II changed our theoretical understandings of the
church, but the older structures have continued to exist. Vatican
II insisted on the church as the people of God, but our structures
do not give enough of a role to all the people of God. Vatican II
emphasised the role of the local church and the collegiality of all
bishops with the Bishop of Rome, but the present structures still
see the church as centralised in the Vatican. A much greater role
must be given to the local, national, and regional levels of the
church universal.

The latest incident with Seán Fagan reminds us of the many
changes that must take place in the way in which the hierarchical magisterium functions in the church. Here, too, the magisterium must recognise the roles of the whole people of God and
of the particular and local churches. History shows us that the
hierarchical magisterium has had to learn before it can teach.
Such a learning process is especially true in the area of moral issues that depend so much on the experience of the whole church.
The hierarchical magisterium must recognise that the teaching
on specific moral issues belongs to the category of non-infallible
teaching – in other words it is fallible. Above all, the hierarchical
teaching office must acknowledge that in the past its teachings
have been wrong and have changed. Think of all the changes
that have occurred in areas such as interest taking, the meaning
of marital sexuality, capital punishment, the right of the defen-
dant not to incriminate oneself, religious freedom, democracy,
and many other areas.[19] The whole church has learned from the
experience of Christian people even though such experience at
times has been wrong, as illustrated in the case of slavery.

Yes, we badly need a change of structures in the church
today, but structural change will not be a panacea. Think of the
problems in the Anglican church today even though that church
has much more participatory structures. We need better structures, but such structures will never solve all our problems and
tensions.

We who work for reform in the church will always know the eschatological tension between the now and the fullness of the reign of God. The church, like ourselves as individuals, will always fall short and be a sinful church. As we are called to be more faithful followers of Jesus in our personal lives, so too we are called to be a more faithful community of the disciples of Jesus. Our Catholic tradition provides some ways and directions for working for change in the church. In this process we reformers must also avoid the danger of writing off or putting down those who disagree with us. The pilgrim and sinful church will always know the tensions of trying to do the truth in love.

CHAPTER THREE

Scribalism in the church

Wilfrid J. Harrington OP

When invited to contribute to this honouring of Seán Fagan, it was proposed that I might revisit an article of thirty years ago, 'Scribalism in the church'.[1] I note that the relevant volume (1973) of *Doctrine & Life* carried an article by Seán Fagan, 'Sacraments in the spiritual life.' Both Seán and I had been earlier, and continued to be, regular contributors. What a glorious time it was, that aftermath of Vatican II. How sad that a determined policy of restoration has led to the dullness and defeatism of today. Happily, the windows that John XXIII opened cannot, despite determined attempts, be slammed shut again. To vary the metaphor, that seed of Vatican II has grown into a tree – a tree now in its winter. It waits to blossom bravely in the spring of a more hopeful climate.

A critique

The drift of my 1973 article was, to begin with, a critique of pre-Vatican II practice and of neo-scholastic theology.[2] Some excerpts will convey its flavour:

> I have noted, for some time now, a strange and disturbing feature. What Jesus has to say about the conduct of his disciples is regularly unambiguous and very pointed. What disturbs me is the discovery of what seems to be an inflexible rule. Simply stated, it is this: the clearer the words of Jesus in regard to Christian conduct, the more certainly have Christians done exactly the opposite! Once I had noted the pattern I could see that the rule had been followed with quite impressive fidelity (p 298).

I have subsequently taken to referring to this phenomenon as 'Harrington's Law.' The text of the 1973 article continues:

The most glaring inconsistency of all is that between Jesus' teaching on the exercise of authority in his church and the actual manner of its exercise. It is remarkable how many times his statements on authority are recorded:

But Jesus called them to him and said, 'You know that the rulers of the Gentiles lord it over them, and their great ones are tyrants over them. It will not be so among you; but whoever wishes to be great among you, must be your servant, and whoever wishes to be first among you must be your slave; just as the Son of Man came not be served, but to serve, and to give his life a ransom for many. *Mt 20:25-28, cf. Mk 10:42-45.*

But you are not to be called rabbi, for you have one teacher, and you are all students. And call no one your father on earth, for you have one Father – the one in heaven. Nor are you to be called instructors, for you have one instructor, the Messiah. The greatest among you will be your servant. All who exalt themselves will be humbled, and all who humble themselves will be exalted. *Mt 23:8-12.*

He sat down, called the twelve, and said to them, 'Whoever wants to be first must be last of all and servant of all.' *Mk 9:35.*

But he said to them, 'The kings of the Gentiles lord it over them; and those in authority over them are called benefactors. But not so with you; rather the greatest among you must become like the youngest, and the leader like one who serves. For who is greater, the one who is at the table or the one who serves? Is it not the one at the table? But I am among you as one who serves.' *Lk 22:25-27.*

After he had washed their feet, had put on his robe, and had returned to the table, he said to them, 'Do you know what I have done to you? You call me Teacher and Lord – and you are right, for that is what I am. So if I, your Lord and Teacher, have washed your feet, you also ought to wash one another's feet. For I have set you an example, that you also should do as I have done to you. *Jn 13:12-15.*

Could anything be clearer? Yet, how easily we have taken over the trappings and the titles and the style of the Roman Empire and, later, of feudalism! Nor was the style of authority in the least affected by a fulsome title such as *Servus servorum Dei*, 'servant of the servants of God' or the like ... Authority in the church has been officially stamped as *diakonia* (service) and, to some small extent, it has begun to look a little like service. The trend must continue; the area for change is wider than we may have realised. And it must continue because of the hardy constitution of a tendency (or spirit) that one may term 'scribalism' which could block – perhaps even reverse – the trend (pp 299-300).

Pharisees and scribes

One section of my earlier article calls for a revision in light of later studies; it is that on 'The Scribes,' touching on scribes and Pharisees in the New Testament, specifically in the gospels (pp 300-301). This was the prelude to a consideration of 'scribalism' in the church. A more careful treatment of the gospel data is called for. It is now manifest that the gospel presentation of Pharisees and, more notably, of scribes is far removed from the real picture. We shall see why this is so. To appreciate the purpose it is helpful to sketch our current assessment of Pharisees and scribes at the time of Jesus.

Pharisees

The Pharisees seem to have had their origin in a religious and political response to the policy of Hellenisation launched by Antiochus IV (175-163 BCE), king of the Asian Seleucid kingdom, and his Jewish supporters. In furthering his policy of imposing Greek cultural and religious practices, he launched an official persecution of the Jewish religion and profaned the Temple by setting up an altar to Zeus. The Pharisees formed a religious and political grouping of devout Jews who perceived a threat to the very existence of Jews as a distinct ethnic, cultural and religious entity. They emphasised detailed study and obser-

vance of the Law of Moses. Besides, they also possessed a normative body of tradition – the traditions of the 'fathers' or 'elders.'
While they acknowledged that some of these legal rules and
practices went beyond the Law, they maintained that such practices were, nevertheless, God's will for Israel. They actively engaged in trying to convince ordinary Jews to observe these
Pharisaic practices in their daily life. Much of what is attributed
to Pharisaic teaching refers to legal rulings or opinions regarding concrete behaviour (*halakoth*) in matters of purity rules, sabbath observance, tithing, marriage and divorce. The Pharisees
lacked political power but would have had some political influence. As a major religious force, they enjoyed the respect of the
people. After 70 CE and the destruction of the Temple in
Jerusalem by the Romans, as practically the only religious group
to have survived the Jewish War, their influence would have increased.

All four gospels attest to frequent contact of Jesus with
Pharisees throughout his ministry. This relationship was, not
surprisingly, one of tension because he and they addressed the
same constituency. He and they sought to influence the main
body of Palestinian Jews and win them to their respective visions
of what God was calling Israel to be. Jesus would have challenged
them directly and in parable. In prophetic mode, he may have
pronounced woes against them. Yet the gospels acknowledge
that some Pharisees were willing to give Jesus a serious hearing
(e.g. Lk 7:36-50; Jn 3:1-2). Their relationship would have been
notably less hostile than represented in Mt 23. [3]

Scribes
The emergence of writing is the obvious starting point for
scribes. The word 'scribe' in Hebrew, Greek and other languages
had a wide range of meaning, open to change over time and
open to a variety of social roles. The range is not unlike that of
'secretary,' which can reach from a minor job in a business office
to a Secretary of State. Scribes functioned in the ancient Near
East over millennia. They wrote, copied and guarded records for

tax and military purposes, annals for government archives and religious texts. They also could, and did, produce literary work. In general, however, they functioned within bureaucratic systems.

Palestinian scribes in Jesus' time were, in fact, bureaucrats. In Jerusalem they assisted the priests in judicial and religious proceedings in the Sanhedrin. They would have played a secretarial role and, as in a modern civil service, some might have had a measure of influence. On the whole, they were 'retainers'. John Meier puts it bluntly: 'That the Jewish scribes were a homogenous religious group with a unified theological agenda as well as with a distinct power base, a homogenous group that formed part of the united front against Jesus, is hopelessly wrong.'[4] We need to see why the gospel presentation of scribes and Pharisees would suggest a different story. We concentrate on the gospel of Matthew. It is noteworthy, however, that Pharisees are practically absent in all gospel passion narratives. This, at least, is historical. The death of Jesus was brought about, not by Pharisees, but by a religious and political alliance of Jerusalem priesthood and Roman political authority.

Matthew
In the decade 80-90 CE, a Jewish-Christian theologian – traditionally we name him Matthew – made a synthesis of the gospel of Mark and a source subsequently named Q. (Q was the name given to a collection of Jesus' sayings. It was not a single document, but more of a tradition that existed among the followers of Jesus. Q comes from the German word *Quelle* which means source or spring). Matthew's community, likely based in Antioch in Syria, was in a crisis situation. It had been a wholly Jewish community tolerated within Judaism, but now, after the destruction of Jerusalem in 70 CE, and the reorganisation of a shattered Judaism, it had broken with official Judaism. As a Jewish Christian, writing out of, and for, a Jewish Christian community, Matthew, like all Jews, had to face up to a radical challenge to Jewish identity. There were stark questions: Where is Israel now? Who is heir to the biblical promises?

The Jewish Christian, Matthew, wrote a Christian gospel. For him, as for Paul, the hope of Israel was in Jesus Christ. However, his post-70 CE situation was not the same as that of Paul. The apostle, whose writings date from around 50-55 CE, was wholly convinced that Israel had not been, because it never could be, set aside (see Rom 9-11). Matthew, immersed in the conflict situation after 70 CE, was not so sanguine. For him, official Judaism was the enemy. In his day, the powerful priesthood had been obliterated. Pharisees were his target, his *bête noir*. His polemical stance is understandable in the context of his situation. Taken out of context it has proved disastrous. His chapter 23, above all, has led to a practically universal characterisation of Pharisees as 'hypocrites' which was grossly unfair. There has been a sad failing in perception. In Matthew's world, ethnic Jews, both Christian and non-Christian, were in conflict. There was no love lost. But this was not anti-Semitism.

Matthew does not hide his bias. He does *not* like Pharisees. One feels that what more seriously disturbed him was the discernment of 'Pharisees' within his own community. It is in one way ironical that this traditionally stolid ecclesiastical gospel, is really subversive of 'ecclesiasticism'. I have often thought that a high-point of ecclesiastical 'hard neck' is the proclamation of Mt 23:1-7 at Sunday Mass – without embarrassment or apology! When one really looks at this passage, and contrasts the practice of the Christian church over the centuries, one must feel some dismay:

> Then Jesus said to the crowds and to his disciples, 'The scribes and the Pharisees sit on Moses' seat; therefore, do whatever they teach you and follow it; but do not do as they do, for they do not practise what they teach. They tie up heavy burdens, hard to bear, and lay them on the shoulders of others; but they themselves are unwilling to lift a finger to move them. They do all their deeds to be seen by others; for they make their phylacteries broad and their fringes long. They love to have the place of honour at banquets and the best seats in the synagogues, and to be greeted with respect

in the market-places, and to have people call them rabbi. Mt
23:1-7.

Scribes and Pharisees

Matthew, a Jewish Christian, would surely have known the status
of Pharisees and scribes. Yet his presentation of them is quite unhistorical (apart from the absence of Pharisees in his passion narrative). We must presume that he knew what he was about. He
pairs Pharisees and scribes without regard for differences. For
him, 'scribes and Pharisees' represent the opposition: official
Judaism ranged against his Christian community. In similar
fashion, the fourth evangelist referred to his opponents as 'the
Jews'. For Matthew, however, 'scribes and Pharisees' were not
only the opposition. More importantly, the phrase also embraces a tendency within his Christian community. This is the
aspect we would develop here.

Conflict between the Jewish authorities and Jesus is well doc-
umented in the gospels. But Matthew 23 is something special.
As it stands, it is an indictment of Pharisaic Judaism, painfully
reflecting the bitter estrangement of church and synagogue towards the close of the first century CE. Yet, Matthew also instances
'scribes and Pharisees' as the negative side of Christian leadership: 'Jesus said to the crowds and to his disciples' (23:1). The
scribes and Pharisees are criticised because their interpretation
of law takes little account of human frailty and tends to be more
severe than humane: 'They tie up heavy burdens, hard to bear,
and lay them on the shoulders of others; but they themselves are
unwilling to lift a finger to move them' (v 4). One thinks, in the
contemporary situation, of male celibates laying down rules for
the married and, unilaterally, defining the role of women.
Matthew continues with his 'scribes and Pharisees': they are
people who make custom their dictator, vanity and ostentation
their lifestyle. Showing off, parading piety, enjoying the lime-
light, insisting on places of honour – these are forms of play-acting,
incredible performances in the name of religion (vv 5-7). How
painfully representative of ecclesiastical style, even to our day.

Happily, it is taking something of a beating. But can there be, against the starkness of the Cross, any justification for silly titles and bizarre garb? And, notably among younger clergy today, there is a disturbing preoccupation with dress.

In Matthew 3:1-7 Jesus castigates the Pharisees and scribes in the third person – 'they'. Then in 23:8-12 he changes to the second person – 'you'; he addresses the church. Matthew's word to leaders in his community is: you must remember that you are servants of the community (v 11). You must avoid the titles 'rabbi', 'father', 'teacher'. The title Rabbi – literally, 'my great one' – would sit incongruously on one who is a 'slave' (*doulos*, vv 20-27) of the community. Nor is anyone to be addressed as 'teacher' – practically the same as 'rabbi'. Though the title 'rabbi' ceased to be used among Christians, the traditional semitic title 'father' became common. Already, by Matthew's time, religious leaders were seeking to be 'real' leaders. True religion as taught and exemplified by Jesus is a family-of-God affair, characterised by simplicity, affection, brother/sisterhood (23:8-12). What he was insisting on – and this is what his followers were meant to be aware of – is that the teacher is the minister and servant of God's word to the people. There is only one Father, God, and all humans are brothers and sisters. There ought not be an insistence on privilege and an exercise of power that distort this relationship. We observe an ironical twist in Matthew's graphic narrative of Jesus' denunciation of those in authority in the synagogue. He is concerned that, in his day, Jesus' followers have developed attitudes and behaviour reminiscent of those Pharisees and scribes. In depicting Jesus' staunch rejection of such conduct, he unmasks the problematic character of leadership in Christian communities. Daniel Harrington comments: 'The prophetic warnings of Jesus in Mt 23:13-31 can serve as a checklist for all who exercise leadership in church or synagogue. Excessive casuistry, misplaced priorities, over-emphasis on externals, etc. are found in every religious denomination.'[5] As for the exercise of authority, Matthew 23 shows, eloquently, how it is not to be exercised. Jesus had stood authority on its head:

exousia (authority) is shown to be *diakonia* (service). Yet, already by Matthew's day, Christian leaders were sporting titles and flexing ecclesiastical muscle.

Scribalism

For a perception of what I have termed 'scribalism' I return to my 1973 article. There I identified neo-scholastic theology as the characteristic theology of scribalism. The period of neo-scholasticism in Roman Catholicism has been incisively surveyed by Mark Schoof:[6]

> In the nineteenth century, neo-scholasticism became the one 'official' school of theology in the Roman Catholic Church, for this was the era of the 'alliance' between the *magisterium*, the teaching office, and neo-scholasticism. In face of that formidable alliance the theology of renewal, due to the efforts of theologians seeking a creative Catholic theology, could not but make heavy weather. Neo-scholastic theology had become the one criterion of theological orthodoxy. Thus, it was assumed, any approach to the reality of faith guided by any other system or idea which did not square with the scholastic tradition must be firmly denied and rejected. This theology had an effective built-in obstacle to any real development: the neo-scholastic theory of knowledge, which lacked sensitivity to history, could find little place for development or adaptation within the neat logical relationships of formalised scholastic concepts. 'The theologians who aimed at renewal had therefore to try to make their efforts acceptable to a teaching authority which knew itself to be at one in this identification of a system of thought and revelation with the overwhelming majority of the church, in which "confusion" was not allowed to prevail'...[7] Happily there were *other* theologians and, unexpected as it must have seemed, their work was not in vain. For the church's teaching office ultimately came to accept the direction in which the theologians of renewal had been moving when, as Schoof aptly puts it, 'the magisterium of the church finally terminated its exclus-

ive contract with neo-scholasticism at the Second Vatican Council.[8] (p 302).

Today we are aware that neo-scholasticism 'hasn't gone away, you know'. It is discernible in the spate of documents emanating from the Roman curia. This neo-scholastic mindset displays a characteristic intolerance of other theologies. There is no place for 'dissent' – meaning, in practice, a choice of a theological alternative. And, in the practical sphere, rules and regulations have again become supremely important.

Religion

'Scribalism' as I have described it in my earlier article and as I propose it here, is a feature of any highly structured religious system. It is regularly to be found among the functionaries of the system. We have seen that, historically in the Jewish world of Jesus' day, scribes were bureaucrats, marginal figures. In the gospels, however, they are said to have a power-base and to be arbiters of theology. Ironically, this unhistorical role became, in time, a reality in the Roman church. The Roman curia is a bureaucracy. Yet, it has arrogated to itself powers beyond bureaucracy. It can, and does, dictate to bishops – ostensibly, the leaders of the church. This is a view forcefully expressed in 1999 by a giant of the Second Vatican Council, the late Cardinal Franz König:

> Within the Catholic church itself no one has difficulties about the existence of the Petrine office, served by the necessary bureaucracy adjusted in line with the times. What is often felt to be defective is the present style of leadership practised by the authorities in the Roman curia dealing with the diverse and multiple dioceses throughout the world …

In the post-conciliar period, as bishops have not infrequently pointed out, the Vatican authorities have striven to take back autonomy and central leadership for themselves …

> [The church] is no longer Europe-centred … we must decentralise. The Roman curia remains a powerful force tending in the opposite direction, towards centralism … in fact, *de*

facto and not *de jure*, intentionally or unintentionally, the curial authorities working in conjunction with the pope, have appropriated the tasks of the episcopal college. It is they who now carry out all of them ...

Today, we have an inflated centralism ... We have to return to the decentralised form of the church's command structure as practised in earlier centuries. That, for the world church, is the dictate of today.[9]

The fatal indictment of this control-driven 'scribal' system comes from the Lord of the church. In a statement that rings with startling authenticity because it runs quite counter to the accepted view of his day, Jesus declared: 'The Sabbath was made for humankind, not humankind for the Sabbath' (Mk 2:27). Here 'sabbath' is code for religion. The declaration sounds: religion is for men and women; men and women are not slaves of religion. This is the radical challenge to scribalism.

Wherever religion is burden, wherever it shows lack of respect for human freedom, it has become oppressor, not servant. Authentic religion must foster freedom. Of course, one has to understand freedom correctly. In a Christian context, freedom is never licence to do as one pleases. Paradoxically, the ultimate freedom is the freedom to serve: 'The Son of Man came not to be served but to serve, and to give his life as a ransom for many' (Mk 10:45). Here is the sure christological basis of true freedom. Religion is oriented to salvation. Salvation is the whole liberation of the wholly human.

What needs to be clearly understood is that a religious system, any religious system, is a human construct. As such it is always open to criticism – in particular, to self-criticism: *Ecclesia semper purificanda* (the church must be continually purified).[10] One can forgive a certain reluctance to embrace the *Ecclesia semper reformanda* (the churh is always in need of renewal) of the Reformers. The difference in formulation is not significant. More importantly, the *semper purificanda* (continual purification) is a healthy and welcome retreat from unrealistic triumphalism.

In Christianity, true religion should operate under the rule of

Christ. Edward Schillebeeckx has observed: 'I recall a splendid interpretation by Thomas Aquinas of what the "rule of Christ" involves. He writes: "The power and rule of Christ over human beings is exercised by truth, justice and above all by love..."[11] Where the church of Christ lays claim to another rule, it does not simply depart from the spirit of freedom, the Spirit of Jesus Christ, but it also fails in its duty towards the world, namely to proclaim and practise the liberating power of the Christian message credibly and understandably.'[12] A church inspired by love is a serving church. In a serving church there is no room for self-righteousness, there is no place for arrogance. There ought to be a place for compassion. There ought to be a place for justice.

Conclusion

My earlier 1973 article concludes:

> In the new atmosphere of today it is so liberating to realise that, after all, there is more than one school of theology. It is so refreshing to make decisions for oneself. But it is wise, too, to recognise that this scribalism is a sturdy plant. If it has been plucked up (or has it?) its roots are still there. It could well spring up again; we must be on our guard. One thing is certain, those who have escaped from its influence and have found freedom will never go back to it, because we cannot. (p 304)

If that 'sturdy plant' has indeed come to life, and some would say that it has, it has not succeeded in smothering theological freedom. In the field of moral theology, at present the danger area, theologians of vision have, courageously, faced and continue to face in realistic and sympathetic fashion, the moral problems of our day. One who surely does so is Seán Fagan, a theologian wholly imbued with the spirit of Vatican II – a theologian internationally respected. He has greatly helped and comforted – and liberated – many. I salute him, my colleague and friend. His writings have reinforced my conviction that the supreme law is the Law of Christ – the 'law' who is Christ.

CHAPTER FOUR

Rosmini, Newman
and the American Catholic crisis

Michael Glazier

Antonio Rosmini (1797-1855) and John Henry Newman (1801-90) are two prophetic voices for the laity from the bleak decades of the nineteenth-century, an era when theological rigidity fostered intolerance and ruined careers. While the ardent and sincere supporters of papal infallibility justified their right to dominate and direct all aspects of Catholic theology, they also felt that history should be an ally of their theology and ecclesiastical politics. They doctored church history. In his landmark and magisterial study, *The Conciliarist tradition: constitutionalism in the Catholic church 1300-1870* (Oxford, 2003), Francis Oakley repairs history, showing how ultramontanist theologians and historians tidied up the Catholic past by diluting the significance of centuries of conciliar theology and disregarding untidy or embarrassing historical anomalies.

Councils Vatican I (1869-70) and Vatican II (1962-5) have come and gone since Rosmini and Newman broke the ice and put the question of the laity on the table in an era when ultramontanists equated orthodoxy with their theology and their view of history. The first council defined papal infallibility and centralised ecclesiastical decision-making in the Vatican; but the second ushered in an era of hope, reform and new horizons, but it did not foresee that its reforms could be delayed, derailed, or vitiated because the council did not reform the Roman curia, which with its innate censorious outlook – unchanged since the days of Newman and Rosmini – is as conservatively powerful today as it ever has been. With a flawed understanding of America and with grudging appreciation of the extraordinary achievements of American Catholicism, the curia in the last twenty-five years has created an American hierarchy in its own image; and an educated laity now openly questions and disputes the Vatican (and the hierarchy) on some focal decisions and positions that intimately affect their lives. (Some in the curia see the need for change, but they are not the decision-makers.)

Rosmini: The prophetic insider

Antonio Rosmini was born into an aristocratic family in Rovereto, Trentino in 1797. Against his parents' wishes, he studied for the priesthood and was ordained at the age of 24. He was an intellectual with wide interests in mathematics, languages, education, philosophy, patristics and all branches of theology. A man of prayer and thoughtful observation, he became keenly aware that the church was ignoring the cultural and political changes transforming Europe. He discussed this with close friends who included nationalists such as Count Camillo Cavour, novelist Alessandro Manzoni, and some learned diplomats and ecclesiastics.

His intellectual abilities were recognised and admired in papal circles and three popes – Pius VIII (1829-30); Gregory XVI (1831-46) and Pius IX (1846-78) – encouraged him to initiate a revival of philosophy and theology in Italy. While he wrote prodigiously, he was dedicated to a spiritual renewal and in 1828 founded the Institute of Charity (Rosminians) which attracted a phalanx of talented recruits. In the 1830s he began assigning small groups of his followers, including Luigi Gentili, to work in England. Their apostolate eventually touched the lives of the clergy and laity throughout the English-speaking world as they energetically promoted the use of the Roman collar and the wearing of the soutane. They also popularised the May devotions, the Forty Hours, the wearing of scapulars and the blessing of throats on the feast of St Blaise.

Rosmini, an uncomfortable insider, felt that the church should not continue to criticise and condemn the social and nationalist revolutions sweeping Italy and Europe while ignoring its own shortcomings. In 1832 he began writing *The Five wounds of the church* and completed this well-structured work of 165 numbered paragraphs within a year. Though a friend of Pope Gregory XVI, he knew that the book would offend the conservative pope who, despite his work for the missions and his condemnation of slavery and the slave trade, was hostile to change and out of touch with the temper of his time and was alienated from the aspirations of so many European Catholics. The pontiff was hostile to all movements of national emancipation. (He even issued an encyclical damning Catholic Poland's revolt against the Tsar.) He surrounded himself with reactionary advisors such as Cardinals Benelli and Lambruschini and he resisted any liberal reforms in the ill-governed and oppressive Papal States. Rosmini had just finished *The Five wounds of the church* when Gregory's *Mirari vos* condemned freedom of conscience and of the press and the separation of church and state. So Rosmini wisely put his manuscript on the shelf and waited for a more suitable and tolerant time for publication.

He waited almost fourteen years until Pius IX was elected in 1846. Here was a seemingly congenial and moderate progressive man, popular with Italian nationalists. So Rosmini published his book privately and distributed it to friends who shared his concerns for the deficiencies in the church. But the book was pirated and was widely circulated. A storm of protest arose from curial circles, and a stunned Rosmini amended some passages in the book and he faintly tried to disclaim that he had offered specific remedies for church reform. 'The aim of the book was simply to point to the agony of the church. Remedies were touched upon only incidentally, and would require a separate study.' Today *The Five wounds of the church* would not raise a fuss, but in the oppressive era of Pius IX, who had shed all liberal leanings, the book blighted the career of Rosmini and he became a listed suspect.

Rosmini's call for five reforms was essentially a plea for a new ecclesiology. His first complaint deplores the completely passive role of the laity in all liturgical functions, especially at the eucharistic celebration. The people did not know Latin, and for many, with little education, the ritual was almost meaning-less. While he did not specifically call for the use of the vernacu-lar, he laid down all the reasons why the laity would benefit by it. His second plea is for an educated clergy, something most Italian Catholics would agree with as qualified and dedicated priests were an exception rather than the norm. In his third call for reform he very diplomatically criticises the hierarchy with great circumlocution. He points to the bishops of the early church, who were concerned for the welfare of the whole church, not just for their individual jurisdictions; and he also ad-verts to the laity's role in nominating bishops. He enumerates several historical trends and debilitating practices – such as the state's intervention in ecclesiastic appointments and affairs and the involvement of bishops, often titled, in secular affairs and politics – that tended to fracture episcopal unity and common concerns. His fourth complaint musters cogent arguments why the state should have no right to nominate bishops. Here again he recalls that in the early church the laity participated in the nomination of bishops. His final 'wound' argues that the church should be free to use its properties and bequests for the good and the needs of its people and that secular authorities should not financially participate in, or interfere with, the church's work in this area. During a pontificate when criticism was al-most treasonous, Rosmini stood alone in Rome and called for changes and suffered for his stand.

At this time, Italy was in political turmoil, and matters were not going well for Pius IX either, because of his insistence that the papal territories were outside the ambit of Italian unific-ation. His prime minister had been murdered in November 1848 and an economic collapse made matters worse. Fearing the anger of the Roman people, he fled to Gaeta, south of Naples. Surprisingly, Rosmini was invited to travel with the pope's en-tourage, but in Gaeta some papal confidants turned on him and upbraided him for *The Five wounds of the church* and for the liberal political ideas in his latest book *La Costituzione secondo la giustizia sociale*. Amazed by the discourtesy and the antagonism he en-

countered, Rosmini decided to return alone to Rome. On his
way back, he was informed that the Congregation of the Index
had secretly held an 'extraordinary' session in Naples and
placed his latest book and *The Five wounds of the church* on the
Index of Forbidden Books. There they remained until Paul VI
abolished the Index in 1966. (Ironically he called *The Five wounds*
'a prophetic work'). But Rosmini's antagonists pursued him,
and thirty two years after his death the Holy Office condemned
forty propositions found in his philosophical works. That condemnation was only lifted by the Congregation for the Doctrine
of Faith on 1 July 2001. When asked how propositions which
were erroneous in 1896 were orthodox in 2001, Cardinal
Ratzinger gave a less-than–convincing response. And in 1998
Pope John Paul II also lauded the life and the works of Rosmini,
whose basic credo was simple: 'All the faithful – clergy and people – represent and form in the church the marvellous unity indicated by Christ ...' (*The Five wounds of the church,* par 15). Long
before Rosmini's name was known outside Italy, *The Five
wounds of the church* influenced John Henry Newman, whose
career was also ruined by pleading the cause of the laity in a landmark essay 'On consulting the faithful in matters of doctrine'.

Newman: the prophetic outsider
John Henry Newman's life was marked by great ideas that
failed. After his misadventure to found a Catholic university in
Dublin (1854-57), Newman looked forward to a period of quiet
study, prayer, and writing. His dealing with the Irish bishops
perplexed him, and he was especially mystified by Cardinal
Cullen's policy of not answering correspondence either to avoid
giving an opinion or to let Newman know his displeasure for
one reason or another. (The English hierarchy, as Newman was
to learn, adeptly used the same tactics, part of their Roman education.) Newman's dream of a studious life was short-lived. On
his return to Birmingham, he reminded Cardinal Wiseman that
Bishop Ullathorne had informed him in 1855 that the Synod of
Bishops had designated Newman to undertake a new trans-

lation of the bible but he had heard no more. Wiseman replied and informed him that Rome had approved the project, but a cat-and-mouse game then ensued on how the project would be financed. Meantime, news came that the Archbishop of Baltimore was working on a new translation and was willing to co-operate with the English project. Newman was enthusiastic; Wiseman withheld his opinion. In 1859 when Newman unwillingly got involved with *The Rambler*, the distrust of the hierarchy and indecision of Wiseman killed the idea of a new translation of the bible.

In 1859 at the behest of Cardinal Wiseman and Bishop Ullathorne and at the urgent pleading of the editors, Richard Simpson and Sir John Acton, Newman most reluctantly agreed to become editor of *The Rambler* to save the lay-run journal from condemnation by the bishops. It had been founded ten years previously by an Oxford convert J. M. Capes, who felt that a high quality journal, owned and run by lay men and completely independent of the hierarchy, would help to win a more acceptable place for the Roman Catholic church in English life. Richard Simpson, another Oxford convert, became the active editor. In 1857 Sir John Acton at the age of twenty-three invested in the journal and also became editorially involved. Acton felt that respectful and open dissent would foster a mature Catholic laity on which the church's future depended.

Before long the hierarchy was fuming because *The Rambler* took it upon itself to offer opinions on the Catholic position on the Newcastle Commission which the government appointed in 1858 to suggest how to extend a sound and cheap elementary education to all classes of children, including those in Catholic and other denominational schools. The bishops had privately decided to ignore the Commission, but *The Rambler* was unaware of this and took the liberty of inviting Nasmyth Scott Stokes, an expert on government educational policy and a distinguished lawyer-convert, to write on the subject. In the January and February issues of 1859, Stokes cogently argued that Catholic schools would benefit greatly by co-operating with

the Commission as subsidies were involved, and if the bishops
refused to co-operate they should be aware of the consequences.
He pointed out that government representatives (not inspectors)
should be accepted in Catholic schools, as they would not interfere with the content of religious instruction. He sided with
Orestes Brownson's position in a similar American school controversy. Brownson argued that it would be better for a poor
Catholic child to attend a well-run public state school, even
when reading the King James bible was mandatory, rather than
be a pupil in an under-funded Catholic school with ill-paid and
half-educated teachers who were hardly qualified to teach the
rudiments of the faith to a child. Cardinal Wiseman and Bishop
Ullathorne, who had hitherto kept silent on their decision not to
support the Newcastle Commission, considered condemning
The Rambler, and thus hastening its demise. But they paused
briefly, and decided to ask Newman to take over the editorial in
the belief that he would make it a respectable and tame publication. Independently, the beleaguered editors also begged
Newman to take the editorial reins and save the journal. On 21
March 1859 a downcast Newman accepted the editorship 'as a
bitter penance'.

In the May issue of *The Rambler* a quieter tone pervaded and
its detractors combed every paragraph for errors, or worse.
Deep in the small type of the double-columned Commentary,
unsigned but written by Newman, were two sentences on the
Royal Commission's proposals on elementary education.
Newman respectfully pointed out that the bishops should have
the opinion of the laity on the education of their children in
which they are deeply involved and concerned. He recalled that
the faithful were consulted prior to the definition of the
Immaculate Conception and that it was natural that they would
be consulted 'in great practical matters' such as elementary
education. In the same issue the adverse judgement reached
secretly by the bishops (the previous November) was published
together with cogent argument by Bishop Ullathorne against
allowing government representatives in Catholic schools. In a

letter to Simpson, Bishop Ullathorne had already made the episcopal position clear: '… it is absolutely unnecessary that the reasons for our own actions should be explained and that the
Catholic community should be informed of the grounds for our
proceedings.' Ullathorne met Newman on May 22 and told him
that the May issue of *The Rambler* was offensive, and he ignored
Newman's response and pleas. Newman then reminded him
that he did not seek the editorship, and Ullathorne abruptly said
'Why not give it up'? Taken aback, Newman agreed and, as
never before became convinced that, with the Roman mentality,
the English bishops regarded the laity as a kind of 'children eternal' rather than as partners with a right to be consulted in matters within their competency.

Before departing, Newman wrote in the July issue his great
essay 'On consulting the faithful in matters of doctrine'. This
was more than a salvo at the prevailing ecclesiology; it was one
of the great theological contributions from the nineteenth-century.
It showed that during the Arian heresy, the faithful preserved
the faith while the pope and bishops argued and vacillated. A
deluge of episcopal criticism rained on Newman. Bishop Brown
of Newport delated him to Rome. Word spread that Newman
had lapsed into heresy and was described in Rome as 'the most
dangerous man in England'. His career in the church was ruined
and for the next thirty years he was distrusted and maligned.
Bewildered by the unending charges and calls for clarification
which dragged on for years, Newman commented '… in former
times there was not the extreme centralisation that is now in use
… There was a true private judgement in the primitive and medieval schools – there are no schools now, no private judgement
(in the religious sense of the phrase), no freedom, that is, of opinion. There is no exercise of the intellect.' Two Vatican Councils
have come and gone since Newman wrote these words. Some
things have changed, others have not. This is aptly noted in a recent issue of *America* (October 4, 2004) by Robert P. Maloney CM,
who served two terms as superior general of the Congregation
of the Mission in Rome: 'Perhaps part of the problem today is

the lack of channels for speaking, especially for lay people ...
Theologians might address difficult issues by publishing articles. But the number and prestige of those summoned by the
Congregation for the Doctrine of the Faith in recent decades
tend to discourage critical public theological reflection.' Rosmini
and Newman could have written these sentences.

Some wounds of the church in America
In 2004 it is estimated there were 66 million Catholics in
America, comprising 23.4 per cent of the population. But when
the approximately 13 million illegal Latino aliens are counted, it
is obvious that one-in-four of all American residents is Catholic.
The perennial sacrifice of American Catholics is illustrated by
their commitment to Catholic education. They support 7,000 elementary schools with over 2 million students; and their 1,350
high-schools educate over 695,000 adolescents. Their college
and university system is unique in the history of the church: 240
colleges and universities cater to 750,000 young women and
men. John Henry Newman's great dream for an educated laity
has been realised in America.

Yet there is a growing sense of alienation from the magisterium
among American Catholics and a deep belief that structural
changes in the governance of the church are overdue. There are
several reasons for this season of discontent, but one obvious
factor is the treatment of women. There are more American
Catholic women than men and it is forecast that in the foreseeable future there will be more women than men graduating
from Catholic centres of higher learning. Today American
Catholics are convinced that women have been consigned to a
secondary role in the liturgical and administrative life of the
church. (There is no doubt that in recent years many women, especially nuns, have taken over key positions in some dioceses;
but generally that would not have happened if qualified priests
were available to fill the posts.) Consequently, lofty papal and
curial statements on the dignity of women get less than scant
attention because they change nothing. Catholics voice their

concerns because they love their church, and silence would be disloyalty.

Background to Vatican II

To put the present situation in a proper historical perspective it is helpful to glance at some focal American/Vatican encounters from 1899 to the present. In 1899 Leo XIII issued *Testem Benevolentiae* condemning a nebulous heresy popularly called Americanism. It was the first expression of the Vatican's distrust of American Catholicism. Then in 1907 Pius X issued his catch-all encyclical *Pascendi* which sweepingly condemned Modernism; and three years later the Oath against Modernism was made obligatory for all priests. These papal actions became the major debilitating obstacles to Catholic intellectual life in America for the next half-century. The few American scholars – such as theologian John Courtney Murray and biblical scholar Edward Siegman – who gained some prominence in these bleak years incurred the disapproval of the Holy Office, which used every manoeuvre to silence and sideline them.

When, on 13 January 1959 John XXIII announced his intention to summon an ecumenical council, Americans did not know what to expect. Some theologians felt that it would be a continuation of Vatican I, but others were simply sceptical. This writer remembers asking the opinion of the Jesuit scholar Martin D'Arcy in New York and was tartly told that the idea of a council was the act of a kindly old man and would end with a whimper. In Rome the curia took control of all conciliar preparations, appointed the ten preparatory commissions and four secretariats to draft documents for the bishops to consider; and decided on a tight agenda. Thus the will of the curia would dominate the council, which opened on 11 October 1962. But on 13 October, the curia was awestruck when Cardinals Achille Liénart of Lille and Joseph Frings of Cologne (whose personal theologian was Joseph Ratzinger) torpedoed the curia's plans by demanding that the bishops should appoint members to all bodies designated to draft documents for the bishops' consideration. That night

Pope John agreed, and the gates of reform were opened. The council lasted until September 14, 1965 and in that relatively short time wonders were accomplished. The church learned to view the work of other churches in a more nuanced, humbler and sympathetic way; it faced the need for reform in the church; and it saw the need to elevate the responsibility of the local churches. In four sessions the mission of the church was reviewed, and the council produced sixteen major documents that constitute in themselves a Magna Carta for the church and are a splendid course in theology for the modern world. Vatican II revitalised all aspects of American Catholic life, and a sense of hope and renewal permeated its activities. Of course there were lively disputes on the scope of reform, but Catholics generally saw great horizons for the church with its new openness and exuberant confidence. But the era of euphoria came to a halt on 25 July 1968 when Pope Paul VI issued *Humanae Vitae*, his last and fateful encyclical.

Humanae Vitae

Pope Paul VI had removed discussion of artificial birth control from consideration by the council and in 1964 he appointed a commission, which included some married men and women, to advise on the question. Among the American members were Patrick and Patricia Crowley, founders of the international Catholic Family Movement, and John Noonan, legal scholar and the recognised authority on the history of contraception. The committee deliberated for three years and overwhelmingly advised the Holy Father that the church should revise its teaching on artificial birth control. But Paul VI, a deeply spiritual but hesitant man, was in a quandary. With his respect for tradition, and influenced by the Roman curia and the writings on love and sexuality by Karol Wojtyla, Bishop of Krakow, the pope rejected his committee's counsel. *Humanae Vitae* created a storm in the Catholic world and American Catholics expressed their disappointment and disillusionment. Sociologist Rev Andrew Greeley succinctly describes the aftermath:

In the confusion, disappointment and anger that followed Pope Paul's *Humanae Vitae* (1968) laity and clergy embraced the principle of following one's conscience. It was this development, more than any other, that shattered the authority structure ... In the late 1960s and early 1970s every segment of Catholic America changed its conviction about the legitimacy of birth control and, more ominously, about the right of the church to lay down rules for sexual behaviour. Authority was no longer centralised; it had become pluralistic. Similarly the acceptance of papal infallibility fell 22 per cent in the United States.[1]

The non-reception of *Humanae Vitae* occurred because the vast majority of the laity and the clergy found its arguments unconvincing, and it opened the way for serious questioning of many aspects of the Vatican position on sexual morality. Many believe that the encyclical, based primarily on natural law, would have been transformed by absorbing the experience, conscience, and wisdom of Catholic parents.

Women's dissent

The curia's prevailing attitude toward women is epitomised in a minor directive of decades ago. The Constitution on the Liturgy (*Sacrosanctum Concilium*) opened the way for lay lectors at Mass. But in 1970 and 1975 the curia made a distinction on how men and women were to exercise ministry: men were to read within the sanctuary, but women lectors were to read outside the sanctuary. Apart from the curia, nobody was surprised by the uproar that ensued and the regulation was reluctantly dropped. Women were further disenchanted by the curia's prolonged opposition to female altar servers. Such insensitivity fostered the rise of Catholic feminism in the United States, an offshoot of the secular feminist movement of the 1960s and after. The latter sought for equal rights for women in civil society, but Catholic feminists demanded fair play and equality in their own church. Women asked why they could not be ordained to the priesthood. With little fanfare Paul VI said it was unfeasible, and the

Congregation for the Doctrine of the Faith issued *Inter Insigniores* (1976), which admitted that there was no scriptural basis for or against the ordination of women, and essentially argued that the priest acts *in persona Christi* and as Christ was male therefore all priests should be male. The argument was not convincing. American women firmly believe that the magisterium – the pope acting with the bishops – is necessary and is designated to teach, but they also believe that the magisterium should listen before it teaches. As the call for ordination continued to grow louder, Pope John Paul II determinedly decided to remove the question from all consideration and discussion. In *Ordinatio Sacerdotalis* (1994), the pope ruled out any possibility of women's ordination; and he had his decision incorporated into the Code of Canon Law. Furthermore Cardinal Ratzinger announced that the pope's position was to be 'held definitively' by the faithful (1995). But the pope went one step further: he firmly forbade any further discussion of women's ordination. Free speech is a pillar of American life and the pope's prohibition of open discussion led many to ask: Do the Holy Father's splendid philosophical expositions on freedom and human rights apply to Catholic women?

Some stalwarts hope that the Vatican will at least restore the deaconate for women, a fluctuating ministry which, though censured by the Council of Nicea in 325 CE, lingered on to the tenth century. But most women are more than dubious, finally convinced that no change can be expected until there are administrative and structural reforms. For openers, they are convinced that the College of Cardinals should be reformed, arguing that it would be a far better and more representative advisory body if it contained some experienced and educated lay women and men. After all, the College survived having a 17-year-old Cardinal Cesare Borgia and a 15-year-old Cardinal Innocenza del Monte, both of whom had violent lives and deaths!

For over forty years Catholic feminists have waged an uphill battle for inclusive or gender-neutral language in public prayer and scripture translations used in liturgy, hymns, preaching, pastoral letters and much more besides. Significant progress has been made and in 1990, the American bishops – in co-operation with bishops throughout the English-speaking world – approved criteria for inclusive language in biblical texts used in the liturgy. For ten years biblical scholars, liturgists and literary experts worked with ICEL (The International Commission on English in the Liturgy) to create translations which were not only accurate but would also have a sense of beauty and liturgical refinement for use in the English-speaking countries. But in 2001, the Vatican issued *Liturgiam Anthenticam*, which rejected the work of a decade and made clear that only literal translations, without inclusive language, would be accepted. Educated Catholics generally – not only feminist activists – were numbed by the curia's lack of pastoral and literary sensitivity. But this was nothing new. Some recalled that Rome delayed the publication of the *Catechism of the Catholic Church* for two years because of inclusive language. A completely new translation was made and approved; but nobody has ever claimed that the *Catechism*, particularly its introductory matter, served the English language well.

The scandal and the bishops

It is not unusual for accusations of child molestation in their homes, schools, summer camps, kindergartens and elsewhere to make headline news on a fairly regular basis, and people ruefully accept that sexual abuse of the innocent is the dark side of the human condition. Periodically a clergyman from mainline churches makes the news, but the most sensational sexual scandals whirl around famed celebrity televangelists such as Jim Bekker and Jimmy Swaggert whose names were almost part of American life. The celibate Catholic clergy were highly admired as pillars of propriety. But in January 2002 *The Boston Globe* broke a story on sexual abuse that stunned America, infuriated the Catholic laity and most of the diocesan clergy. Eventually the bishops in every diocese of the United States were in the dock of public opinion. *The Boston Globe* showed that Cardinal

Bernard Law, the most powerful figure in the hierarchy, had failed to protect children and teenagers from sexually predatory priests. The investigative reporters dug up facts and also had solid confidential data from within Law's inner circle. The habit of quietly moving predatory priests from one parish to another, without informing the new parishes, became the accepted practice. Some became notorious national figures. For example, the unfortunate Boston predator Father John Geoghan abused children in parish after parish, and was eventually murdered in prison. As more and more victims came forward, many clergy took leave of absence. Law faced the rising scandal and outrage with fortitude and arrogance. He was forced out by an outraged laity backed by a disillusioned clergy. Cardinal Law was the Vatican's man; on his word bishops were appointed, disregarding the wishes of the local clergy and laity. After *The Boston Globe*'s revelations, papers across the country, from *The New York Times* to *The Los Angeles Times*, joined in an unprecedented investigative crusade and it became obvious that every diocese was involved in the covert scandal. The faithful felt betrayed, stunned by the whole hierarchy's pattern of cover-up, secrecy, complicity, hush payments and callousness toward the victims over many years. Catholics are indebted to the secular media for breaking the cover-up of long-term sexual abuse by priests. Yet some conservative spokesmen righteously condemn their thorough investigative work; but they don't ask why 167 diocesan newspapers, controlled by the bishops, kept silent.

The low point in the history of the American hierarchy came in June 2000 when they assembled in Dallas and sat in silence while their leadership was questioned, and sexual abuse victims related the damage wrought to their lives by clerical abuse and its cover-up. So the humiliated bishops had no option but to accept a Charter for the Protection of Children and Young People that would be operative in every diocese. They also agreed to the formation of a lay National Review Board to monitor the bishops' compliance to their commitment to establish procedures to protect children and teenagers against molestation by members of the clergy and by people employed in schools or connected in any way with diocesan activities. The National Review Board employed a firm comprised mostly of former FBI agents to audit the compliance of each diocese; and in 2004 they reported back that the majority had complied with the Charter's provisions. The Board had also commissioned the John Jay School of Criminal Justice to conduct a wide diocesan investigation to ascertain the number of priests accused of the sexual abuse of minors since 1950; to accumulate data on the victims; and to reckon the money expended to date on settlements and for treatment of victims and priests. The inquiry discovered that 4 percent of all priests, since 1950, had perpetrated acts of sexual abuse primarily against male children and teenagers. But it noted that not all victims had come forward. By the spring of 2005, the American Catholic community had to pay almost a billion dollars in compensation to victims and for legal fees. But that is only the beginning and the clock is still ticking and payments will continue to be made for years to come. The financial holdings of most dioceses are tightly-kept secrets; but new organisations such as The Voice of the Faithful ('Keep the faith, change the church') are now insisting that the Catholic people have a right to know how their money is managed.

Good men, flawed leaders
The National Review Board also sought to get an insight into the root causes of the scandal by conducting extensive interviews; and its report focuses on church leadership in America. It accuses the bishops of failing to recognise the scope of the problem and of ignoring warning signs available to them in 1985 and before. It shows that they were more interested in saving face than in the devastation caused to so many young victims. Some bishops regularly used legal tactics to avoid pastoral responsibilities; and most evaded reporting sexual crimes to the legal authorities. The investigation indicated that few bishops felt they were accountable to the pastors of the parishes or to the laity. Thus it became almost natural for them to wrap embarrassing situations of their own making in a shroud of secrecy.

In his book *A People adrift: the crisis of the Roman Catholic Church in America*, Peter Steinfels analyses the bothered and bewildered American church.[2] While he points to the wonderful vibrancy, versatility and achievements of the church, he intimates that the Roman curia has put the American hierarchy on a tight leash. Steinfels rightly asserts that generally the bishops are good men and adds 'Of course there are exceptions, but mediocrity, not malevolence, is the more typical espicopal infirmity.' The pastoral tragedy is that the faithful lost trust in their bishops in the midst of an unprecedented vocation crisis. Today there are only 35 replacements for every 100 priests who die or are completely retired, and that number is forecast to decline further and faster. Over the last twenty-five years, Pope John Paul II has shown that he does not favor a decentralised administration, and no bishop has been ordained who didn't show absolute loyalty to the papal position on *Humanae Vitae*, abortion and the ordination of women. And, consequently, no seminary professor has been appointed who was unwilling to swear the same allegiance. In the long run, this policy fosters alienation rather than orthodoxy, because neither the faithful's rejection of *Humanae Vitae* nor their inability to be convinced by the arguments against women's ordination will go quietly into the night.

When one tries to trace and map the root causes of the crisis in American Catholicism, it becomes clear that most roads lead to Rome. Yet those who feel obliged to constructively criticise the administration of their church do so because they love it. They believe that the Holy Spirit will calm the troubled waters; and while they see a dark-clouded horizon they confidently and optimistically utter: 'This too shall pass'.

CHAPTER FIVE

Spiritual abuse

Seán Fagan SM

The sexual abuse scandal is the biggest crisis to hit the Catholic church in a very long time. It was a major blow to people's faith that priests and religious could abuse their power to harm innocent young children, ruining their lives, and in some cases even driving them to suicide. It is small consolation to discover that in the United States most churches accused of this abuse are Protestant, or that 85 per cent of abuses take place in families, by babysitters, neighbours, family friends or relatives. But the bigger scandal, which has totally shocked Catholics, is the failure of church leaders to cope in a gospel way with the problem. Bishops who for years ignored accusations or even knowingly shuffled abusers to fresh pastures have not been asked to resign. The first reaction of some Vatican cardinals was to say that it was only an American phenomenon or that homosexuality was the cause and that homosexuals should never be ordained. Prodded by the media spotlight, the institutional church is at last, however slowly, facing up to the problem.

But there is another abuse that has not received the same amount of publicity, but affects a much greater number of people. It is a moral disease that has affected the church for centuries. It can rightly be described as spiritual abuse. It is no mere dis-ease leaving people uneasy in one or more areas of their lives, but a deep-down illness which damaged their emotional and spiritual lives, leaving them with huge burdens of unhealthy guilt. So many older Catholics find it hard to experience the joy and hope *(Gaudium et Spes)* that the Vatican II document on *The Church in the Modern World* is so excited about. They may read the words, but there is little joy in their hearts, because so much of their religion was a matter of duty and obligation. They learned this from Holy Mother church, in spite of the challenging words of Jesus condemning the Jewish leaders for laying such heavy burdens on people without ever lifting a finger to help them.

Fr Donal Dorr is a highly-respected world class theologian who wrote about this problem with great insight and feeling, describing his own experience of how the church's spiritual abuse affected his life.[1] His reflections on the problem made him more and more aware of the layers of confusion that surround the issue. The present writer is totally in agreement with his basic argument, though reflecting a somewhat different personal experience. Ordained in 1953, I have been teaching moral theology (as well as philosophy, scripture and some canon law) in Dublin since 1955. At intervals since 1960 I have taught moral theology and spirituality to international renewal groups of priests, nuns and brothers in Europe, Asia, Africa and North America. For the past fifty-one years I have heard confessions and given spiritual direction in twelve countries of widely different languages and culture. What I most remember from all of this is the enormity of the harm done to Catholics by what we now realise was the spiritual abuse practised unknowingly by the church for centuries. After several hours in the confessional on a Saturday night (with penitents who confessed weekly or monthly) I often came out on the verge of tears, thinking: what in God's name have we done with people's consciences?

One of the great blessings of my life was that I seem to have missed the fear and scrupulosity that marked the lives of so many people, both growing up and into adult years. From infancy my God was the loving God of infinite compassion, who smiled on his creation, one who did not have to close his eyes or turn his back when I took a bath or discovered that I was a sexual being convinced that the female human body is the most beautiful of all God's wonderful creations. I sat through many hell-fire sermons and retreats and listened to all the warnings, but they never bothered me seriously, although they reminded me that I could mess up my life and hurt people by not keeping close to God. Hell fire was certainly in the background, but I never thought that large numbers of people, if indeed anybody, would be punished in that way. Even as a teenager, when I read of saints who spoke of souls dropping into hell like leaves in wintry weather, I was annoyed, but I simply felt that one could be a canonisable saint and still talk nonsense.

Sexual morality

When studying moral theology I was fascinated by the logic of it all, but felt that the treatment of sexuality and marriage was wooden and unreal, at times almost revolting. In some English language text books the more intimate details were in Latin. I wondered about the psychological make-up of celibate clerics who could picture, analyse and measure the weirdest details of sexual deviations. Their texts nowadays seem to border on the pornographic. For the morality of sex, the basic principle was that all directly voluntary sexual pleasure is mortally sinful outside of matrimony. This meant that for a single act of teenage self-gratification one would be condemned to hell for all eternity. People were led to believe this, and had to live with the fear. Unlike all other areas of morality, where the seriousness of a sin may be lessened by smallness of matter, even the slightest experience of sex was matter for mortal sin. I was never convinced of the reasons for this and never accepted it, but it was imposed by authority and most people felt obliged by it. I taught it simply as a matter of history, but could never convince students that it was true. Truth cannot be decreed or imposed, but only discovered and shared. Only later, in the ministry of counselling and in the confessional did I realise the enormity of the burden of fear and guilt people developed as a result of this teaching. For decades I seldom heard confessions without 'bad thoughts' being mentioned as a sin, and over three quarters of men confessed 'self-abuse' as a mortal sin keeping them from Communion, even though most of them were devout Catholics, quite saintly in every other area of their lives.

Until the mid-80s I knew about paedophilia as a psychological phenomenon, and I was vaguely aware that some men 'tam-
pered with little boys' but, like most of the population, I was unaware that large numbers of people suffered child abuse as we
know it now. It was never mentioned in confession by either
perpetrators or victims, and I think that few victims were able to
reveal it, so one can hardly speak of a 'conspiracy' of silence.
Most people were simply unaware of the abuse unless they had
personal experience of it. I doubt if police or social workers
knew much more. For centuries moral theologians listed the
major sexual sins as: fornication, adultery, rape, abduction, in-
cest, sacrilege (sex with vowed religious), sodomy, and bestiality.
These were analysed in terms of what was natural and appropriate, just or unjust, but the age of the victim was never a factor of
importance. Child abuse was not a special category because it
was not recognised as such, and hardly anybody knew that the
practice was so widespread, or so devastating in its consequences. The early sex scandals that brought shame (and criminal charges) to priests and religious around the world were not
always about child abuse. But the publicity and court proceedings in such cases encouraged victims of child abuse to speak
out, and more people have found the courage to come forward.
Since then I have listened in counselling sessions to many victims and I become more and more horrified at the enormity of
the harm done. Some extreme cases may be driven to suicide,
but very many are emotionally and spiritually crippled for life.
They can be helped by counselling, but it is a slow and painful
process, and there is no guarantee of total success. Financial
compensation can never make up for what the victims suffer.
The church must name this evil as a special sin in a category of
its own, and wherever church individuals or institutions are
even slightly implicated they must accept their responsibility
and ask forgiveness. The victims need this to begin their healing.

Spiritual abuse
It is clear that child abuse is not a new phenomenon, but an evil

that seems to be part of our flawed human condition. Because of the taboo surrounding sex it was not generally recognised or discussed, so that it is only in recent years that we have become aware of its malice and its crippling effects. The same may be said of the spiritual abuse that has crippled generations of Catholics. Novelist David Lodge gives a sadly funny description of the almost permanently tormented state of a pubescent young Catholic male's conscience.[2] Just as victims of sex abuse find it almost impossible ever to feel 'happy in their own skin,' huge numbers of Catholics find it difficult to experience the joy and inner freedom that Jesus promised his followers. It is now generally recognised that sex abuse is more an abuse of power than of sex, and in a similar way it can be said that the spiritual abuse that is a disease in the church is an abuse of power and authority and not simply the result of ignorance. For centuries, a certain type of church teaching, instead of setting people free to grow into the fullness and maturity of Christ (Eph 4:13), kept them enslaved by a childish conscience forever in dread of hell for all eternity. This fear was particularly felt in the area of sexuality. Text books were unanimous in describing 'company keeping' (even in preparation for marriage) as a necessary occasion of sin, and marriage itself was such a minefield that it was almost impossible for married couples to avoid sin. The charismatic renewal movement helped many people towards some degree of joy in their religion, but it seldom went to the root of their agony and fear by questioning the ignorance, prejudice and appalling theology on which the common teaching was based. The church was the absolute authority, speaking in God's name.

When the church spoke in God's name it had no direct communication from him. It had the Word of God in the books of the bible, but these are all in human words. There is no word of God in pure unadulterated form, a-temporal and a-cultural. The word of God comes to us in human words, and every word from the moment when humans first learned to speak is culturally conditioned, reflecting the experience and culture of the speakers. The biblical descriptions of the creation of the world and the beginnings of the human race are not historical facts, literally true, but stories that teach profound religious truths dressed in the simple thought-patterns of primitive people. The picture of God is quite savage at times, unlike the God who is the Father of Jesus. He exhorts his people to slaughter their enemies in thousands, and he has no objection to slavery and polygamy. Throughout the bible there is growth and development in moral sensitivity, but there are also huge blind spots. St Paul is quite lyrical about all people being equal, so that there is neither Greek nor Jew, male nor female, slave nor free person, and yet he saw no reason ever to question the institution of slavery as a natural part of the social order and indeed of God's will. We have learned to accept this cultural conditioning of God's word expressed in human terms, and we make the necessary distinctions. But cultural conditioning did not stop with the bible. Every word and thought of the church over two millennia is subject to the same cultural conditioning. The science of hermeneutics enables us to interpret documents to discover their full meaning. Women theologians quickly recognise the cultural background of the Vatican's male, celibate, clerical world where there is no significant female presence, and at times they see it as closed and narrow, cut off from the wider world of the ordinary people who are the vast majority of the members of the church.

Cultural conditioning

We can understand cultural conditioning as a normal part of history, but can we be sure that some of the attitudes in the past that we are now ashamed of are not still at work in our collective subconscious? Has the misogynism that was a feature of the church for centuries been admitted and repented of? Church leaders can be patronising in hesitantly admitting that women may have got a raw deal in the past, but most men have no idea of how deeply women feel about the injustice they still suffer today. Can it be said that the words of leading theologians and some saints for centuries in the past had nothing to do with modern attitudes to women? A few examples: Clement of Alexandria: a woman should cover her head with shame at the thought that she is a woman. St John Chrysostom (died 407): woman is a necessary evil. St Jerome (died 420): women are the gate of hell. St Augustine (died 430): women are not made in the image of God. Pope St Gregory the Great (died 604): woman's use is two-fold: animal sex and motherhood. St John Damascene (died 750): woman is a sick she-ass ... a hideous tape-worm ... the advance-post of hell. St Thomas Aquinas (died 1274): woman is an incomplete being ... a misbegotten male. Pope John XXII (died 1334): woman is more bitter than death. St Albert the Great (died 1280) was not only a bishop and a theologian, but also a scientist who wrote volumes on astronomy, chemistry, geography and physiology, who was canonised in 1931 by Pius XI and proclaimed a Doctor of the Church. He repeated Aristotle's teaching that woman is a misbegotten male with a faulty and defective nature compared to man's. He said that 'she is unsure of herself, and what she herself cannot get she seeks to obtain through lying and diabolical deceptions. To put it briefly, one must be on guard with every woman, as if she were a poisonous snake and the horned devil.'

It is naïve to imagine that this kind of thinking and language had no influence on church teaching and practice. No matter how much the ideal of Christian marriage was preached, ordinary people, both women and men, were deeply affected in their spirituality by the pessimism concerning sex. According to Augustine, only procreation could justify marriage, sex, or even women. Pope St Gregory the Great claimed that it was as impossible to have intercourse without sin as it was to fall into a fire and not burn. Clement of Alexandria compared marital intercourse to 'an incurable disease, a minor epilepsy'. St Jerome, who translated the bible into Latin, held that virginity was the norm in paradise, that marriage came about as a result of sin, and that the only good in marriage is that it can give birth to virgins. In the fifteenth century St Bernardine of Siena, one of the greatest preachers in Europe at the time, claimed that 'of 1000

marriages 999 are of the devil's making.' He also maintained
that it was a piggish irreverence and a mortal sin if husband and
wife do not abstain from intercourse for several days before re-
ceiving Holy Communion. For centuries it was church teaching
that women should not be baptised when pregnant or during
their monthly periods, and they were not allowed to enter
churches or receive communion at those times. The ritual impurity
incurred by women at childbirth was accepted until quite recent
times (in the 'churching' ceremony). This notion of ritual impurity infiltrated Christian thinking and legislation from pagan
superstition, according to which terrible things were believed to
happen when women touched anything during their periods:
crops would dry up, fruit rot on the trees, and iron would turn
rusty. It is easy to smile at such thinking today, but it is hard to
avoid the impression that the negative attitude that permeated
Catholic moral theology for centuries still lurks behind church
teaching on women. Modern women are not shy in dismissing
the nonsense of some Vatican documents, but Christian women
for centuries were psychologically and spiritually crucified by
the way they were spoken about and treated.[3]

Authority and influence – or power and control
Church leaders are conscious of their authority, and ideally their
pastoral ministry is modelled on Jesus, who 'spoke with authority' and had tremendous moral influence. But what many of the
faithful experience on the part of church leaders is primarily a
concern with power and control, with little reference to the
gospel. How many bishops ever wondered why for decades
huge numbers of Catholic married women abstained totally
from Communion between the ages of 25 and 45? Responsible
parenthood forced them to use artificial contraception. It was
church teaching on birth control that cut them off from full sharing in the Eucharist. When the Second Vatican Council discussed marriage, Pope Paul VI reserved the question to himself
because he wished to hear the results of the special papal commission established to advise him. This group, of six people at

first, but then enlarged to 58 in 1965 and then 72 in 1966, were mostly on the side of the official teaching at first but at the end of its work concluded almost unanimously that artificial contraception was quite lawful. Only four members, priests, took the opposite view, in favour of the traditional teaching, but they admitted that their position could not be theologically proved, that it was really a matter of authority; if the teaching were changed it would lead to a major schism in the church, and the church cannot admit that it ever made mistakes. The commission saw three thousand letters from Catholic married couples in eighteen countries describing their experience, against the traditional teaching. The pope ignored all this evidence. There is no proof that he ever even saw it, and the Vatican has not allowed it to be published. It is claimed that Pope Paul VI had the special assistance of the Holy Spirit in writing the encyclical, but it is difficult to understand how he could hear the voice of the Holy Spirit in the four clerics who told him what he wanted to hear, when he never consulted the solemn assembly of the world's bishops in General Council discerning the good of the church, and he rejected the near-unanimous vote of his special commission on the subject as well as the thousands of letters from married couples, all of whom are temples of the Holy Spirit, who speaks through their lives, their experience and their faith. In matters of faith the pope can only define what is already the faith of the church. This does not seem to be the case in matters outside the realm of faith.

A church that is so obsessed with authority loses credibility when it massively ignores the authority of the facts. It conveniently forgets the many dreadful things that were proclaimed for centuries as the 'teaching of the church,' but which nobody can accept today. To take an example from living memory, Pius XI in an encyclical on Christian education (with the same level of authority as *Humanae Vitae*) solemnly declared that 'co-education is erroneous and pernicious, and is often based on a naturalism which denies original sin … Nature itself, which makes the two sexes different in organism, inclinations and attitudes, provides no argument for mixing them promiscuously, much less educating them together.' Catholics are confused by this and wonder how the 39-year interval between the two encyclicals (1929, 1968) allows us to treat one as a museum piece quietly forgotten and the other as a serious obligation in conscience, indeed in some cases an impossible burden for responsible parents. Is this not a further reminder that all doctrinal statements, like the bible itself, are historically and culturally conditioned? No statement from the past is set in stone, and it cannot be proved that the church never made a mistake.[4] We are all a mixture of saint and sinner, and this applies to the church as institution as much as to its members individually.

Conscience a sanctuary

The narrowness and harshness of church teaching in this area not only left people with sexual hang-ups, but struck at the very core of morality by crippling their conscience. They were always told to follow their conscience, but it was stressed that it had to be an 'informed' conscience, with the implication that the church would give the 'information' on what they were to do. It was never explained that it was not just a matter of information to be supplied by the church. We are to follow a 'formed' conscience, one which is continually being formed through life as we grow in moral maturity, discerning moral values and deciding with full responsibility before God, enlightened by church teaching. People who lived all their lives in the 'do what you are told' church found it hard to believe that the Second Vatican Council, the highest authority in the church with the pope as member, could solemnly teach that conscience is our most secret core, and our sanctuary. There we are alone with God, whose voice echoes in our depths. People would be helped enormously if they felt that the institutional church really believed this in practice.[5] The Vatican Congregation for Divine Worship recently issued new rules for celebrating the Eucharist, the central thrust of which is to stress the sacredness of places, things and people surrounding the Eucharist. The presidential chair is not an ordinary, profane piece of furniture, but a sacred seat for the sacred priest celebrating in the sacred place of the sanctuary. Should we not respect and reverence even more the sanctuary of people's conscience, which is truly sacred? For centuries conscientious objectors to war were ignored or merely tolerated by church authorities, seldom respected as morally responsible people who quite frequently were prophetic in their stance.

Ironically, on the sacredness of conscience, theologian Ratzinger sums up perfectly the teaching of Vatican II: 'Over the pope as the expression of the binding claim of ecclesiastical authority, there still stands one's own conscience, which must be obeyed before all else, even if necessary against the requirement of ecclesiastical authority. This emphasis on the individual, whose conscience confronts him with a supreme and ultimate tribunal, and one which in the last resort is beyond the claim of external social groups, even of the official church, also establishes a principle in opposition to increasing totalitarianism.'[6]

Church leaders were so conscious of being the highest moral authority, acting as the voice of God, that they expected total obedience even in areas in which many of the faithful had far more competence and experience. The Vatican Council acknowledges and respects this competence, which is not limited to secular concerns but is to be seen also in theological and scriptural research and reflection. Many of the writings of women and men theologians frowned on by the church have enriched its health and vitality. Cardinal Newman stressed that infallibility (not a very helpful term) is an attribute of the church as a whole, with the hierarchy (including the pope), theologians and the whole body of the faithful having their appropriate share in it. A sad tendency in some Vatican departments at present is that theology is being reduced to a simplistic 'the pope says'. Intelligent laity have real difficulty in understanding and accepting some of the language used in official documents. Traditional church teaching speaks of contraception, sterilisation, masturbation, direct killing of the innocent, divorce and remarriage as intrinsically evil, as evil in themselves, independently of all circumstances. Few theologians today accept such language, since they know that no physical action on its own can be given a moral label unless seen in its concrete totality with its human meaning, including motive and circumstances. Murder is killing, but not all killing is murder. Lying is telling a falsehood, but not every falsehood is a lie. Contraceptive pills are said to be intrinsically evil, but they were allowed by the Vatican for nuns threatened with rape in the Congo, and *Humanae Vitae* explicitly allows them for thereapeutic reasons, e.g. to regulate the cycle. But all these cases involve the same pills, working in the same way according to God's chemical and physiological laws. Since the main difference is the intention or motive, it cannot be the artificial contraception as such which is evil. If there are exceptions according to motive and circumstances, the description 'intrinsically evil' has little meaning when applied to physical actions. To insist on the use of this language is a failure to respect people's God-given critical intelligence. The Holy See's *Declaration on Abortion* (1974) makes no use of this expression and yet presents a very convincing moral argument, whereas the *Declaration on Sexual Ethics* (1975) uses it freely with reference to masturbation and homosexuality and signally fails to prove its point.

Holy mother church

So much of church teaching in the intimate questions of sexual morality seriously harmed people in their spiritual lives, torturing their conscience and making it difficult for them to realise that our God is a God of infinite love, and that God's love became flesh in the person of Jesus of Nazareth, a human being like us in all things but sin. His total openness to all those he met in his human life is in sharp contrast to the church's exclusiveness. Women are very conscious of being excluded in practice from so many areas of church life, but a much more massive exclusion is that of the laity as a whole, who form 99.9% of church membership. The way in which the church squanders lay experience is an indication of the dysfunctionality of the church as community at the present time. Church leaders seem not to have noticed that huge numbers of lay people are far more theologically literate than many clergy, and are wholeheartedly committed to their Catholic faith, but their experience and their views count for nothing in practice. It can be said in some countries nowadays that most theologically educated Catholics are not clergy.[7] One of the sad consequences of the failure to acknowledge the presence of the Holy Spirit in the faith and experience of God's holy people is the fact that many church documents on sexuality and marriage show little of the ring of truth, theological insight and the flavour of the gospel to be found in Jack Dominian's beautiful book, *Living love – restoring hope in the church* [8] and his many other writings.

Modern theologians try to contextualise their theology (liberation theology, feminist theology, African theology, etc), and we should listen to gay, lesbian and other groups of Catholics. But there is need for an acceptance of all laity as a specific and important group as such, without any implication of inferiority, of passive acceptance as mere recipients of sacraments. If church leaders are not listening to these holy people, each of whom is a temple of the Holy Spirit with personal faith and a wealth of human experience, how can they claim to be listening to the Holy Spirit as they make their pronouncements? The people who write Vatican documents seem imprisoned at times in a rarefied world of neo-scholastic abstractions and often seem to imply that the people they are addressing are somehow inferior.

The Inquisition lives on

Over thirty years ago world-renowned scripture scholar Wilfrid Harrington OP, author of 47 books, wrote about scribalism in the church. He noted that Jesus in the gospels spoke clearly and unambiguously about the conduct he expected of his followers, but the clearer his words the more certainly have Christians through the centuries done exactly the opposite.[9] For many thinking Catholics some of the procedures and practices of the institutional church are a major stumbling block to their faith. First and foremost is the Congregation for the Doctrine of the

Faith (CDF), formerly called the Holy Office, and before that the Inquisition. In the full assembly of the Second Vatican Council Cardinal Frings said that this department of the pope's civil service was a scandal for all Christendom. The eminent and very Catholic historian Eamon Duffy says that 'the establishment, elaboration and privileging of the Inquisition by successive popes, the promulgation of Bulls against heresy and witchcraft, the creation of the Index of Prohibited Books, the shaping of the church's relation to the states of medieval and modern Europe, and the uniform practice of repression and censorship at the heart of the church's own central government – all this surely constitutes more than 'silence' and can hardly be treated as the incidental activity of some of the church's children. Here the church itself is implicated, and here too is something like that structural sin which the pope has discerned in the world's political and economic structures, operating within the heart of the church itself.'[10] During the Council there was a call for a reform of the CDF, but nothing happened, since it continues to operate today in a culture of secrecy and encourages the faithful to spy on fellow members of the church and to denounce them to the local bishop or to Rome. Its procedures have little in common with the openness and fairness of internationally accepted standards. Theologians can still be denounced anonymously to Rome and silenced without a proper hearing. There is a long list of theologians who fell foul of the CDF and were harshly treated. Many of them suffered serious illness as a result of their treatment.[11]

Space does not allow for discussion of other forms of spiritual abuse in our church. For example, there is no convincing theology to justify the following: obligatory celibacy as a condition of ordination for diocesan priests; the refusal to even think of ordaining women to the priesthood in spite of St Paul's insistence that all members of the Body of Christ (Greek and Jew, male and female) are equal in God's eyes; the thousands of Christian communities deprived of the Eucharist for a year or more simply because there are no male celibate clerics to provide the sacrament;

the fact that murderers, serial rapists and paedophile priests have free access to Holy Communion while committed Catholics who have suffered marital breakdown but now find the grace and intimacy of God in a new relationship are forbidden the sacrament; the church's description of the millions of people whom God has made homosexual as 'objectively disordered', and condemning them to celibacy when they have no vocation to it; the absolute condemnation of condoms even when needed by a wife to protect herself from contracting AIDS from her infected husband. There is no revelation of God to support the church's harsh, uncaring attitude towards all these situations, or to justify its refusal to develop a convincing theology that would bring us closer to the gospel in these areas. Is it God's will that huge numbers of God's holy people, temples of the Holy Spirit, are being alienated through no fault of their own from the church they love?

One could continue in this vein, multiplying examples, but the point is clear. Personally I have overwhelming evidence of the harm done to people's emotional and spiritual lives by the abuse of authority and power by our Holy Mother church (with the best of maternal, protective intentions). It is no exaggeration to describe it as spiritual abuse. Much of church teaching stunted their lives. The church has seldom openly and honestly disowned the many terrible things that passed for 'church teaching' over the centuries. In 1431 the illiterate nineteen-year old Joan of Arc was burned at the stake as a heretic, a liar, sorceress, blasphemer, and idolater. Five hundred years later Pope Benedict XV canonised her as a saint. Why does the church need centuries to admit that it was wrong? A little humility and repentance would do far more for its credibility than more solemn documents insisting on its authority and its monopoly of the truth. Jesus did not say that we possess the whole truth, but he promised that his Holy Spirit would lead his followers into all truth.

The Vatican Council brought a wonderful theological and spiritual liberation so that we now give a central place to the notion that our God is an infinitely compassionate and loving God who calls us to respond freely in love to his call. We need to be reminded that we are created in the image of God and that we are most like God in our freedom. If we truly believed this we would have a church of joy and hope, like the big tree mentioned by Jesus, in which all the birds of the air can find shelter. We have had too long a history of exclusion and excommunication. We need to return to the openness, the inner freedom and the joy and hope of the gospel. Large numbers of Catholics around the world are crying out for the affirmation, healing and growth that they have a right to expect from the church which claims to be not only a light to the nations, but also their holy mother.

CHAPTER SIX

The Making of an Irish Catholic journalist

Justine McCarthy

I am descended from a long line of devil's bait. First there was Eve, the protoplasmic human clone spun from a man's rib, whose seduction of Adam doomed mankind to the evil-ever-after of original sin. Salome slithered out of the shadows, slinky as a serpent, for the delectation of her stepfather, and demanded John the Baptist's head on a plate as her prize. Then came Mary Magdalene, the scarlet woman rescued by a divine heart.

These were the stories that nurtured our girlhood. They were populated with dark-eyed sirens luring men into fabulous forests to devour their souls. We girls were born wicked. Our role on earth was to make men stray, though precisely how we were to do this was kept a mystery. It was our nature to serve as Lucifer's man-traps. For we were no more than a defect in the male seed, according to the definer of original sin, St Augustine.

At Corpus Christi, our town would dazzle for the procession. The women spent the weeks before it washing windows and curtains and scrubbing the footpath outside their hall doors where life-size statues of Our Lady and St Michael the Archangel would observe the passing parade. A swirl of girls in frothing communion dresses went by first, their faces veiled and their spindly legs blue with the cold. Next came Canon Butler, vestmentally shimmering beneath a swaying, golden-fringed canopy borne by the altar boys. After that came the men of the town. They wore their suits and pious eyes that could not be deflected from their worship of the middle-distance, singing without joy or musical accompaniment to the Queen of Heaven as they solemn-paced past. Holier than the holiest among these were the nicotine-stained characters who puffed and swore their

way through Sunday Mass, only coming in from outside the front
door to receive and then to flee, jamming the caps they had knelt
one knee upon during the Consecration back on their heads, to
annihilate the first pints pulled in the bars down in the town.

Growing up

My mother has a photograph of me aged about five, standing
outside our front door watching the Corpus Christi procession. I
am wearing a plain, immaculate frock, though my face is
splodged with dirt, and I am standing beside a plaster Virgin
Mary. When we retrieved the picture from the family archives,
my mother passed it to me and wondered: 'What were you
thinking?' Right enough, there is an expression of puzzlement
on that little girl's face. I like to imagine that it was the glaring
inequality of the occasion, or the theatre of a town in cahoots, or
the perplexity of a child's innate sense of fairness that furrowed
my face, but I suspect it was something more important, like
whether it was a sin to have orange swiss roll for tea on Corpus
Christi? I certainly did not have the knowledge to postulate that,
but for the felicity of time and place, the child in the snapshot
could grow up to be declared a witch and burned at the stake. By
the time that photograph was taken, my mother had made a
gently-bold stand against the church's trollopisation of women.
She refused to be churched. Having suffered the ignomy of
purification once, she declined the parish priest's invitation to
what the church characterised as The Thanksgiving of Women
after the births of her three other children. As a consummately
feminine woman, her action was all the more subversive, albeit
devoid of any articulated ideological motivation. She simply
could not bear the humiliation. Following the birth of her first
daughter, she had been summoned to a side altar straight after
12 o'clock Sunday Mass. St Patrick's was still murmuring with
the faithful who lingered. My father had waited in a centre pew
(she was grateful – most husbands left) as the parish priest
sprinkled her with holy water and invoked every saint in God's
kingdom to cleanse her after the dirty business of giving life.

Never again, she vowed afterwards, emboldened by hurt in-
comprehension. 'They tell you it's a sin if you do it before you're
married, and it's a sin if you do it after you're married,' she ful-
minated to my father. I asked her one day, when she was seventy-
eight years old and we were driving somewhere alone, how she
felt when the priest purified her. 'Cheap', she said.

Bandon was a plantation town and religious denomination
ranked high in its pyramid of identity. Back in the mists of history,
an unseen hand had written a prohibition on the town's walls
that neither Jew nor Catholic may enter, to which a visiting Dean
Jonathan Swift had written the rejoinder: 'Whoever wrote this,
wrote it well, for the same is written on the gates of Hell.' The
historical, but non-derogatory, response whenever someone
asked you where you were from was, 'Bandon, where the pigs
are Protestant.' It gave us a distinction. We boasted that we had
nine churches, only one of which was Roman Catholic. There
were Church of Ireland, Presbyterian, Methodist, Quaker,
Baptist, Unitarian and any number of you-name-it religions
scattered in and around our streets. We had a branch of
Cooneyites, who were coffined in my father's undertaker's yard
with the passage to cross the Jordan in pockets specially sewn
into their shrouds. In South Main Street, the shopkeepers' names
above the doors were Jeffers, Goodes, Merricks, Gambles and
Bolsters mingling with Begleys, Mehigans, O'Driscolls, O'Farrells
and Deasys. In early summertime, the town tremoloed with the
pipe-'n'-drum band rehearsing for the Twelfth expedition to the
far-off North. One farm family used to paint the roofs of their
outhouses orange every summer. Yet, there was no overt acri-
mony. Maybe the location of St Patrick's on the hilltop lording it
over the town and its hinterland was as much a site of appease-
ment as of adoration. We children were forbidden to darken the
doors of the other churches. As we grew older and braver and
sneaked our heads round the groaning door of St Peter's whence
we fled in hysterical cry each time we espied the hulking silhou-
ettes of the tombs inside, one thing was clear: hellfire was a
superfluous sanction in keeping us out. Burying your dead in-

doors was infinitely creepier than the hushed confidence that 'the Prods don't believe in the Blessed Virgin'.

Father Christy

Every June, Father Christy came to visit in his black Volkswagen Beetle and would drive us to Coolmaine, where the Bandon nuns had their summerhouse and where he taught us to swim. Sister De Lourdes in our school had warned us that any girl who wore a bikini would burn in hell, but the tinker women in Coolmaine went into the sea in their brassieres and girdles and Father Christy never cast a remark. He was the luminary of our family circle. He had spent a decade ministering in the Australian bush and came home with a trove of stories about kangaroos and flying doctors and hats with bottle corks dangling from them. Some of the older people fawned over him because he was a priest, but he was unalterably humble and never wasteful of words. He was fastidious in his personal hygiene. The black suit and white collar were immaculate and his bespectacled face had that raw, just-washed sheen that I was sure was his soul radiating through his forehead. When our father died of a heart attack in his car at the age of 44, Father Christy became our bedrock. He had baptised all four of us girls with new-fangled names that the parish priest sanctimoniously denounced for the dearth of saintly progenitors, and he would officiate at our weddings, raising no impediment to our mother walking us up the aisle to 'give us away' in our father's absence. After eleven years in a girls' convent boarding school, where the young curate's visits for confessions made the nuns blush, and the walls were plastered with images of Saint Ursula and the vestal virgins, I went to Dublin to study journalism. Father Christy and his trusty Beetle were at the station, both beaming. That Christmas, he brought me to *One Flew Over the Cuckoo's Nest* at the Gaiety Theatre where we shared the cosmopolitan shadows of the dress circle and a box of Black Magic while McMurphy went berserk on stage.

The perils of journalism

Journalism was a fright. It was strewn with hazards. There were clattery old typewriters with banjaxed keys and purple-nosed reporters for whom timidity was an effete condition not to be tolerated in a newspaper office. The spectre of libel lawyers poised to pounce on every dropped comma or misspelt name caused fretful nights and extensive probing of conscience till dawn.

It was exhilarating, except when you wrote anything that impinged on the moral agendas. Then came the twisted, poisonous letters, usually anonymous and pockmarked with hate. These were the years of the abortion and divorce referendums, the Kerry Babies Tribunal, the sacking of a school teacher called Eileen Flynn for living with a married man in Wexford, the awful deaths of Anne Lovett, the 15-year-old schoolgirl, and her newborn baby, found at the Marian grotto in Granard. These were, though most of us did not realise it then, the death throes of a repressive, dictatorial, nation-defining dinosaur fondly known as Holy Catholic Ireland. The secrets kept spewing out. Goldenbridge. Letterfrack. The Magdalene laundries. Bishop Eamonn Casey. Father Michael Cleary. Father Brendan Smyth. Father Sean Fortune. The X Case. The C Case. The babies exported to America for adoption. Every one a skeleton staggering out of a closet that could no longer withstand the strain.

I remember interviewing a man named Alan who had been raped, nearly suffocated to death, photographed *in flagrante delictu*, ritually and systematically sexually attacked and, ultimately, paid off by a priest whose Masses he served as an altar boy in Dublin's Pro-Cathedral in the 1970s. Alan was the most visibly tormented person I have ever met. His need to divulge what had been done to him threatened to be stifled by his equally desperate compulsion to never utter those strangulating words. The most painful thing for Alan was knowing that the priest who had brutalised him was residing at ease in a Dublin parish with the blessing of his bishop, the same man who had provided the money for the compensation payment. My glance kept flitting to the windows of the room where we met to ensure they were locked, because we were three storeys up and I was afraid Alan might try to jump out.

'May you die screaming of AIDS,' wished one correspondent after the interview with Alan was published. 'Last night, I attended my weekly prayer group here in Donegal and I interceded with them when they wanted to have your soul damned for eternity,' wrote another. 'You must mend your pagan ways. I won't always be there to save you.' There were many more letters, with postcodes from every demographic corner of the country, unanimous in their denunciation. Always the presumption was that every 'Dublin journalist' was a trendy, liberal drop-out Catholic on a zealot's mission to wipe out the church. A woman journalist was the ultimate two-headed gorgon – liberal and feminist. 'You and your liberal media cronies made your bed, now lie on it. You reap what you sow. So shut up whingeing.' By the time Mary Robinson went to see the pope in the Vatican on International Women's Day in 1997, wearing an emerald wool suit and a symbolic sprig of mimosa in her lapel, feminism had been so successfully caricatured by Catholic traditionalists that a young priest who branded the presidents' supporters 'Áras-lickers' became something of a pin-up for the holier-than-thous.

Signed letters were unusual. One such, in response to a feature on the demonisation of Annie Murphy, the American-born mother of the Bishop of Galway's son, chastised: 'You do know, don't you, that you will go straight to hell for your anti-Catholic propaganda.' It came from a nun in a prestigious convent school.

Journalism for a Catholic

When my husband's parish priest was handing over the requisite letter of freedom to facilitate our marriage, the elderly cleric idly wondered: 'And who's the lucky girl?' His geniality gave way to vitriol when he learned that the bride-to-be was a journalist. This priest despised the media. Sunday after Sunday, he climbed into his pulpit with his hump of prejudice and castigated journalists as the greatest evil in society. Had I arrived from Mars and been engaged in choosing an organised religion to join, these self-described Catholics would have scared me off their church swifter than anything written in a newspaper. Their interpretation of Christianity was an insult to the man who gave it his name, and who entreated us to love our neighbour. It took a while to understand that it was fear – not loathing – that made them vituperative. The fear manifested itself horribly. One day, I stood in a farmer's field and listened to a powerfully-built tiller of the land recount how one of his daughters had been molested at the altar rails of his church by the parish priest and how his bishop had steadfastly done nothing about it. When another of the man's daughters died in a freak accident after the abuse, some of his Christian neighbours opined, behind his back and in anonymous letters addressed to his home, that it was God's way of exacting retribution for what the farmer had been saying about the priest.

That molten hostility has subsided over the years, to be replaced by the silence of indifference. Church issues occupy fewer and fewer column inches as society grows more secular and the old 'moral agenda' has acquired the irrelevance of a previous generation's concerns. This climate was unimaginable a decade ago. Immigrant workers now provide the backbone of many Sunday congregations while everyone else goes shopping or gets an all-over tan in a spray-on booth. The Taoiseach's acknowledgement that homosexual unions need to be regularised in law barely raises an objection. The erstwhile loquacious bishops, it seems, have taken a vow of public silence. Like the Bounty's mutineers, they have settled for a shrunken pond just as long as they can go on being the big fish.

As the state clanked into action with the Child Abuse Commission, The Redress Board and the Murphy Inquiry into Ferns, more Irish females than ever were giving birth without the benefit of wedlock, more were going to England for abortions, and more still were opting to have their tubes tied. At the same time, fewer men were ordained into the priesthood. What was once the unsurpassable achievement of an Irish mother – to gaze into her son's face and call him Father – decelerated, as if overnight, from a flood into a slow drip. These days, a proud Irish mother waits at the gates of rehab or the graduation hall.

The church's grim determination to ignore the connection between its denigration of women and the decline in its numbers is potentially its own terminal diagnosis. It was women who arranged the flowers on the altar, who housekept for the clergy, who inculcated the reverence for those men of the cloth, who danced tea and cake and fuss upon their visits, who nursed them when they were sick and dying. Women bred them and fed them. It was hearing their children blurt out the festering secrets of priests who destroyed their childhood, (many reiterating in the course of their telling that they could not bear to shatter their mothers' innocence with the necessary harsh, anatomical words) that ruptured the bond of trust. For some of those mothers who still stayed within the fold, trust became impossible once they learned how church elders had covered up and facilitated the abuse of their children. The message was inescapable: chosen sons were reared to be priests; the rest of the boys and girls could be their playthings, while Mother church turned a blind eye. At the time of writing, this institution, which takes the image of the Madonna and child as its very conception, has never said sorry for usurping that fundamental relationship of trust. Occasionally, a bishop or priest raises his head above the parapet to hector the masses for the godless splurge of secularism, as if the people were the shatterers of their own illusions; an exiled laity who had engineered their own alienation. Of the institutional church's own role in exploding trust, there is never a mention. The tenet of confession, that there can be no forgiveness until there is contrition, has become yet another metaphor for one law for the church rulers, another for the rest of us. Faith may be personal, but trust takes two.

Our dysfunctional church

The institutional church's truth dysfunction is the sorriest of the whole sorry shambles. Time after time, it has shown itself to prefer the lie and, still, our spiritual leaders seem not to understand the anguish of betrayal inflicted by their dishonesty. It could not be a greater corruption of a vocation if doctors were discovered murdering patients on operating tables or NGOs were razing seedling crops in famine-stricken countries. When was the last time you saw a cardinal or a bishop cringe as he uttered a patent untruth or half-truth? We have grown as accustomed to ecclesiastical truth-dodging as we have to the banks feathering their offshore nests and politicians hawking their influence.

The relationship between the church and the media is, by the nature of two institutions that see themselves as upholders of the truth, fraught with tension. When neither institution is a saint, that tension inevitably turns to conflict. The church fashions itself as the disseminator of the Good News and, once upon a time, it was the *de facto* editor-in-chief for the nation. Until the late 1980s, the Irish print media ran the gamut of popular press from Dev's *Irish Press* to the Catholic-genuflecting *Irish Independent*. Both toed the hierarchy's line religiously. They supplied a daily diet of moral orthodoxy. Nothing was ever challenged. It was the same in radio and television, where the state broadcaster served as a prism for episcopal optics. The code of omertà remained intact into the early 1990s.

On the morning the story broke in the newspapers about the Bishop of Galway's son, my editor packed me off to the United States to interview Annie Murphy, the boy's mother. Somewhere over the Atlantic, an Aer Lingus stewardess told me cryptically that a message had come through to the cockpit from my office to say that 'your interviewee is on board'. Knowing Annie Murphy was in Connecticut, where we had an appointment to meet at her home the next morning, I guessed the message meant that Bishop Casey was on board. When six Aer Lingus crew members denied he was in the plane and I was barred from ascending to the first-class upper level to check, I returned to my seat. After arrival, of course, it emerged that the bishop had indeed been on that flight (he was whisked on board at Shannon while the rest of the passengers were mandatorily diverted into the terminal building and was magicked off again at JFK, into a waiting car). Nearly a year later journalist Veronica Guerin tracked down Bishop Casey in America and conducted a riveting series of interviews with him for the *Sunday Tribune*. In one instalment, he recalled his flight from Ireland that day with a smug account of how he had eluded a journalist who, he said, had chased him across the ocean. I believe that Eamonn Casey was a victim of an uncompassionate institution that bundled him out of sight that day, but the blend of casual lie and the triumphalism of deceit contained in his account epitomises a cultural ambivalence to the facts that, unfortunately, I have encountered again.

In April 1994 I drove to Wexford for an appointment to interview the Bishop of Ferns, Dr Brendan Comiskey, a media-savvy prince of the church whose fondness for the drink was an open secret, but kept a secret, nonetheless, by a Fourth Estate with a soft spot for mavericks and no stomach for embarrassing the hierarchy. When his housekeeper opened the front door to my ring of the bell around midday, I recognised the bishop instantly – he was the figure staggering drunkenly in the hallway behind her. For the next two hours, he drank whiskey and wine copiously, slurred his speech, made scant sense, staggered when he attempted to walk and swayed when he stood. That night, I rang my editor and told him what had occurred, adding that I did not want to write about it as I believed the bishop was an alcoholic on a bender and that he should not be ridiculed for his illness. I got the impression that, even had I felt compelled to write the truth, the paper was disinclined to publish it. So I wrote a 2,000 word article for the Saturday edition culled from my paltry, bizarre notes. It mostly consisted of meandering descriptions of the bishop's house, clothes and the food on his table in a desperate attempt to fill the page. Throughout the following couple of weeks, missives popped up in the Letters to the Editor page from incensed readers condemning my superficiality in failing to report anything more profound than the colour scheme of the bishop's parlour. The charade was maintained. Some of Dr Comiskey's confidants were aware that the newspaper had not revealed what transpired that day, yet these same people have subsequently, on different occasions, bashed the media for sensationalism and lurid journalism. This surely hovers somewhere near the top of the Richter scale of hypocrisy! When Bishop Comiskey suddenly upped and left the Ferns diocese six months later on a mystery trip to the United States, his brother bishops claimed that he had gone to be treated for diabetes. He was, in fact, in a drying-out clinic for alcoholics. The truism that *in vino veritas* could not be applied to the upper ranks of holy men.

The media are not anti-church

It is a fallacy that the media are anti-church. Yes, there are television programmes and press images and a commentariat that fly in the face of the old strictures and, yes, the church has got a bad press in recent years, but no worse than it merits. If Father Ted is as bad as it gets, the bishops should be counting their blessings. But the siege mentality prevails. Media organisations comprise the same hotchpotches of flawed humanity as other collectives. The disenchantment with the Catholic Church that has been tracked in society is reflected in the media workforce. There are journalists who are scornfully non-religious or anti-religious, as there are journalists who go to Mass every week, who bless themselves when they walk past a church and who are raising their children in the faith, despite everything. It really is time to stop blaming everyone else for the sins of the fathers.

Silence is not an option either. After the fury of the past decade's scandals, the post-storm quiet might be interpreted as harmony. Banish the thought. It is plain couldn't-care-less apathy. The appetite for religious discourse has been blunted by modernity, prosperity and the church's abysmal failure to examine its own soul. Seven years after President McAleese received communion in a Protestant church, it is inconceivable that such an act would trigger the same convulsions. Who wants to get bogged down in transubstantiation when the Vatican is still twitching at the thought of altar girls? After all the anguish and disappointment and bewilderment of the past decade, the church still seems hell bent on unclasping the grip of its surviving members with breath-taking displays of heartlessness. Surely, only a cadre that has learned nothing from the upheaval could endorse a letter such as the *Collaboration of Men and Women*, written by Cardinal Ratzinger in July 2004, enumerating women's contributions to church life as, in brief, being seen and not heard.

The arrogance persists. If the good news is not making headlines that is the failure of a church dominated by a group of men with a mighty superiority complex. Pluralism, like secularism, means it is every interest group for itself now and the Catholic Church is going to have to fight for those column inches of space it appears to believe are its God-given right. The media is big business. It is high time the church leaders climbed down off their pedestals and accepted that the biggest obstacle to getting their thrupenny bit of good publicity is journalism's bottom line: it has to be a good story. In the past decade, while the church has been declining, the media has been growing into a vast, amorphous conglomerate. The thing is not to fear this new monster. Exploit it. The variety of television and radio stations, newspapers and magazines is an open invitation to an organisation with news to spread. So go tell it, because the mountain will not come to Mohammed.

By the time my son was born, Father Christy was aged eighty-two and living with the Augustinian community in Cork. He bought a one-day return train ticket and arrived at Holles Street hospital, bearing two gifts. One was a framed picture of the Mother of Good Counsel. The other was a gold pen. His visit lasted long enough for him to bless the baby and to advise the mother, 'Don't stop the writing.' That exhortation had become his refrain. A man not given to effusiveness, the encouragement he gave was boundless and bold. Whenever I wrote a piece that was critical of the church's status quo, an envelope would arrive in the post days later addressed in Father Christy's familiar, now trembling hand. 'Keep up the writing,' he would cheer. Most people who knew him would have been shocked to know of this quiet rebellion. I was, every time one of those letters came. In all other ways, he presented a model image of the conformist priest. He was holy and gentle but he cared too much about his church to say nothing.

When he died in his sleep in his ninety-first year, his fellow priests found a neatly folded bundle of never-worn clothes at the end of his bed. He had thought of everything. Even in death, he was ensuring that his brothers in Christ would be encumbered with the minimum of preparation for his funeral. If only the church he loved could be as humble.

CHAPTER SEVEN

The Changing concept of marriage and family

Anne Thurston

A middle-aged man stands weeping at a graveside. The 'family', the next-of-kin, are somewhat embarrassed by this show of grief. They have just buried their uncle, their brother, for whom some felt mild affection, others merely the attachment of ties of blood. None of them can imagine what depths of feeling would arouse this display of emotion. Not until many years later would the nephews and nieces come to realise that this bachelor uncle was gay and the man weeping at the graveside was his partner. They never saw him again. The understanding of 'family' was not wide enough to embrace the lover and faithful partner of more than twenty-five years.

Some years after that funeral, a young woman tells her parents that the man with whom she has fallen in love is divorced and has a child. Her mother weeps. The dreams of a wedding for her eldest daughter with all the blessings of the church are shattered. On the day of her marriage the young woman's parents go to Mass while she goes to the registry office. However, they do not withhold their own blessing and later come and celebrate with their daughter and her husband. They never look back and never offer words of recrimination but support the new family in its fragile early days until it becomes strongly rooted. They welcome the child and rejoice in their grandchildren. Through them the young woman learns the meaning of acceptance, the generous and gracious gift of love which bears all things and which endures.

Changes in the shape of family life
A recent article in *The Guardian* newspaper talked about the

dramatic changes in the shape of family life. The writer, Madeleine Bunting, suggested that these changes of the past thirty years will be consolidated in the next two decades. 'All are agreed that by 2020 it will be very difficult to talk of a "typical" family, such will be the variety of shapes and types of families.'[1]

Although Irish society is not as far advanced along the same path it is difficult to believe that the changes will not ultimately be similar. In Britain the married couple with 2.4 children is disappearing and, as Bunting points out, the sequence of life events: marriage, sex, children, has been radically reordered. Cohabitation here in Ireland is becoming the norm and there it has trebled. In Britain the rate of divorce has doubled and the concept of 'serial monogamy' is commonplace. With the introduction of divorce legislation in Ireland this too is becoming more usual. A divorced couple may re-marry their new partners and move in to a complex household of 'his', 'hers' and eventually also 'their' children. These combined families require an exceptional degree of negotiation of roles, and the assumption that the 'romantic' love of the couple will carry them through is misguided, if not dangerous. Step-families are notoriously difficult and it is not without reason that fairy-tales are full of 'wicked step-mothers'! And having been there I know something of that minefield.

The stigmas surrounding divorce and single parenthood have all but disappeared. Bunting predicts that by 2020 children living with both biological parents will be a rarity. She suggests many different types of parenting arrangements with all sorts of combinations of step-families, same-sex couples and, of course, increasing numbers of single parents. The question she poses for us as a society is: how do we view all of this? Do we see it as evidence of a huge moral collapse? Does it mean the complete breakdown of family life? Or could it be seen as a radical re-ordering of relationships still allowing for emotional and societal stability?

Our assumptions about what is normative are based on very recent experience. The notion of romantic love as a basis for marriage, for example, is a very recent phenomenon. The idea of the nuclear family is a contemporary one and, for some, this is clearly a dysfunctional model. We could put these things into question and ask whether there might be other bases for committed relationships. I sat with my niece recently and looked at a family sketchbook belonging to my grandmother and we noticed how there was a sense of a large extended family – in that case involving unmarried aunts, grandparents, nursemaids and so on – creating a kind of small community within the household.

Throughout history marriages have been contracted for purposes which are wider than those of the actual couple and have repercussions for the community – issues of land, the need for an heir, the matter of a dowry, and so on. The emphasis has shifted greatly in our time and culture from marriage as an institution to marriage as an inter-personal relationship.

Interpersonal relationships at the heart of marriage

This change to place the personal relationship at the heart of marriage is good and welcome. It is the understanding of marriage as primarily covenantal rather than contractual, as expressed in Vatican II, which forms the teaching of the church today:

> Married love is an eminently human love because it is an affection between two persons rooted in the will and it embraces the good of the whole person; it can enrich the sentiments of the spirit and their physical expression with a dignity and ennoble them as the special features and manifestations of the friendship proper to marriage …
>
> A love like that, bringing together the human and the divine, leads the partners to a free and mutual self-giving, experienced in tenderness and action, and permeating their entire lives; this love is actually developed and increased by its generous exercise.[2]

The stress has shifted from a reading of marriage as existing primarily for the purposes of procreation to an understanding of marriage as a 'relationship of life-giving love'. In contrast, the Code of Canon Law of 1917 described the primary purpose of marriage as the procreation and education of children. It could be argued then that the understanding of sex has changed from being purely procreational, to relational, and in our time there has been a further shift to an understanding of sex as recreational.

The shift to the personalist understanding has been largely welcomed, without denying the social aspects of marriage. However, I wonder whether we now place too much stress on the personal relationship and whether that might contribute to a situation where all other aspects of marriage are so downplayed as to seem irrelevant. When this wider picture fades, then the couple see marriage as essentially 'their own business'. This must be a contributory reason as to why couples increasingly choose co-habitation over marriage. 'What difference does it make?' they ask, and depending on their attachment or detachment from religious practice, will emphasise either that they feel their love does not need that piece of paper to prove it or they are not interested in having it solemnised. If they do have a wedding, it is essentially an expensive party.

Same sex, same difference?

Against this backdrop it is interesting to consider the desire of same-sex couples[3] to have their unions legally recognised by civil authorities and ritualised by the churches. This should not be looked at in isolation from the general trends. However, there is a certain irony in the situation: same-sex couples seeking recognition and stability for their unions may be counter-cultural and bucking the trend, but not in the sense traditionally understood. As my eighty-year-old aunt from Canada commented wryly, 'Gay couples are the ones queuing up to get married in church, no one else is interested anymore. You'd think the churches would be glad to welcome them!'

It would indeed be ironic if the very groups most interested in demonstrating commitment were the ones barred from expressing it. So we find ourselves asking why? What do these couples feel they need, over and above the personal relationship?

Reading again the definition of marriage as cited in the

Vatican II document, we can certainly see how such couples would want to argue that their understanding of their relationship is the same as that of heterosexual couples: *an eminently human love because it is an affection between two persons rooted in the will and it embraces the good of the whole person; ... A love like that, bringing together the human and the divine, leads the partners to a free and mutual self-giving, experienced in tenderness and action, and permeating their entire lives; this love is actually developed and increased by its generous exercise.* The 'sameness' of experience might seem more relevant than the sameness of the sex of the couple.

The issue of same-sex couples and their unions serves at this time to make us reconsider what marriage is, what purpose it serves and how it might be defined again for this new millennium. In some paradoxical way those who are shifted to the edge of any debate are those who articulate it most forcefully.

All you need is love?
I am going to put into question the received 'wisdom' that all that 'all you need is love'! The singer, Bob Geldof, in a Channel 4 television programme broadcast in Autumn of 2004, expressed deep misgivings about this media-perpetuated myth and argued strongly for a return to real commitment and care to carry a couple through the inevitable difficult times. Both he and the philosopher Alain de Botton argued that while weddings are popular, marriage is not, and that a couple can only feel secure when there is a solemn commitment. I want to suggest that many of the difficulties being endured at the present time in relation to marriage arise from this notion of romantic love which cannot survive the stresses of the reality of living together and bringing up a family.

This is not a plea for a return to the notion of marriage simply as a contract, as institution, but it is a plea to revisit the social aspects of the marriage relationship. At a very basic level some form of contract gives security to the couple, it simplifies issues of sharing property and resources during life, and enables inheritance to pass from one to the other after death. Giving social form to the relationship also provides a more secure environment for any children. Because we have moved to embrace the interpersonal aspect of marriage we may fail to recognise the value of the contractual aspects. Sadly, the only discussion one hears of these at the moment are those pre-nuptial agreements entered into by celebrity spouses which are clearly designed with the presumption that the marriage is a temporary arrangement. It is not a case of who gets what if one dies, but who gets what when they divorce. This aside, there is a value to the notion of contract and, even more so, to the richer idea of covenant which extends beyond the legal requirement to include the notions of love and fidelity. Of course in the Roman Catholic tradition this fidelity is seen as stretching unto death, with the concept of indissolubility. This needs to be re-described as something that is created from within the marriage itself. A good marriage by its nature becomes indissoluble. 'I feel now that I am a part of you,' commented a husband of twenty-five years, to his wife, 'I cannot imagine my life without you. It would be half a life.' The two become one and it is this process of becoming one that creates the indissoluble bonds which 'no person can put asunder' for love has sealed them. This is a far cry from the notion of indissolubility as something imposed from the outside. It is part of the process, the becoming one, which marriage is. It seems to me that it is possible to hold firm to the idea of life-long fidelity, of unconditional commitment, while acknowledging that some marriages fail. The two manifestly do not become one.

Sex as recreation? Sex as re-creation

Reading contemporary theological accounts of marriage I'm struck by the strong emphasis on the personal relationship aspect. Theologians take pains to point up the difference between their approach now and the approach to marriage prior to the modern era when marriage was seen primarily as a biological sexual union entered into for the sole purpose of procreation. Current theology affirms the value of the sexual relationship and extends the notion of life-giving to include the 'life' that one person in the relationship gives to the other. Marriage may, or may not, result in the birth of children who are gift and grace to such a relationship, but may still be described as 'life-giving'. The recreational aspect of sexuality mentioned earlier may be over-emphasised in the media but can be retrieved within a committed relationship to mean precisely what it suggests: a capacity to re-create, to generate love and life. Incidentally, the problem with sex as depicted in the media generally is not that sex is seen simply as recreational – selling everything from ice-cream to kitchen cleaners – but that sex is depicted as an act divorced from a personal relationship. This objectifying of the sexual act makes of it yet another consumer product: 'Did you get any?' is the crude code for this. We live in a highly sexualised but relationally impoverished society. The emphasis is on performance, putting extraordinary pressure on young and vulnerable people who should be free to explore their first fumbling attempts at sexual intimacy in a genuine relationship, not as a test of how 'cool' they are. Failure is labelled as frigidity or impotence, and the young women and men – or more likely girls and boys – are left with their sense of self bruised. They are stripped and they are teased.

We do not know the reasons for the frightening increase in the suicide of young males in particular, but it would not be surprising if one of the contributory factors were the whole issue of sex divorced from relationship. There is little or no opportunity to develop relationships of companionship and growing intimacy before one is expected 'to perform'. In addition to this, some young people may be struggling with questions about their sexual orientation. To come out as gay may be a selling point of reality television, but the prevailing culture remains ambivalent at best, and downright hostile at worst, towards openly gay men and lesbian women.

It is not just the pattern of marriage, sex and children which has changed but the pattern of relationships where sex now precedes friendship which may or may not follow. This is damaging both in heterosexual and homosexual relationships. Friendship is a greatly underestimated source of value and needs much more theological exploration. Friendship should be the firm ground from which relationships grow. Sexuality is the energy which draws people out towards one another, but its expression should be determined by the context. The description in the *Catechism of the Catholic Church* of homosexual acts as 'intrinsically disordered' is decidedly unhelpful as it, too, divorces acts from relationships.[4] It also limits the understanding of life-giving to reproductive life, which does not do justice either to heterosexual or homosexual relationships which may be open to life in many different ways. This possible openness is not helped by closing off such couples, not just from possible sources of support and blessing, but also from the possibility of contributing to the community.

Private weddings, public marriages

The changing culture has altered our view of marriage and put huge pressure on it. I came across a telling comment in an article on marriage: 'Given the lack of external support for marriage provided by society, it is necessary that marriage be held together by values within.'[5] That statement nicely illustrates part of the problem as the writer goes on to talk of the moral responsibility of the couple to do what is necessary 'to maintain vitality in their marriage'. The question I would ask here is whether a couple can be expected to succeed without external supports. A marriage is not simply a declaration in front of one's friends that this union is now official as it were, but it is also an insertion of that union into the community.

There is much discussion at the moment about the fact that religion has become privatised and this is in line with general social trends which are highly individualistic. Contemporary marriage fits the pattern: partners seek self-fulfilment, and if they don't achieve it with one partner they will move on to another. In some ways the over-emphasis in contemporary theology on the inter-personal relationship contributes to this trend. The couple become the centre almost without reference to the wider community. If, from the beginning, there was an understanding of this relationship as set into a network of relationships from which it would derive strength and energy and to which it would contribute life, then there might be less pressure on the couple and their relationship as the only sustaining factor. Paradoxically, some of the very irregularly constituted families in contemporary society might offer some insights. Instead of condemning some of these arrangements, we might look at how they work.

Extending the boundaries
Anecdotal evidence throws up the following contemporary examples of family life. On a television documentary programme a gay Anglican priest describes his 'family': he lives with his partner of twenty-five years, his elderly and disabled mother and a foster child with learning difficulties. I do not know what form of covenant binds these people. However, considering his Christian orientation (of considerably greater importance than his sexual orientation, as Paul reminds us in Galatians 3:27, 'there is no longer Jew or Greek, there is no longer slave or free, there is no longer male or female, for you are all one in Christ Jesus'), I expect that there is a commitment of love and fidelity, not just between the partners, but to the vulnerable old and young in their care. This man considers his set-up as 'a model extended family'.[6]

A few days later I am listening to the radio and hear a woman describe how both she and her partner brought children from previous relationships to their marriage. She speaks of how they worked to bring the children together into a new unit, how the children resisted the attempts of others to sort them out, to see who belonged to which partner, how they invented a composite inclusive name to describe their new belonging, and how eventually they became one family. Sometimes this is a very painful process and sometimes it fails. But it can be observed as a form of community living, which, as such families become more common, will need to be recognised and supported. Once again one could imagine the need for a covenant that would offer a promise to already wounded young people that this new family would try its utmost to be faithful to them, and to protect them, and to create a safe environment in which all could thrive. These reconstituted families cannot take account simply of the needs of the couples, either individually or as a pair. From the start, they come enmeshed in relationships that will impinge on the marriage and therefore that marriage needs to be understood as inclusive of those others. As I suggested, romantic love alone cannot be expected to carry a couple through such a process. On the other hand, a commitment, not just to the relationship, but to the whole family, with a supportive wider network of included extended family could help.

What we might learn from these different forms of family life is the need to look at all families in a wider context so that couples are not isolated in a bubble which will burst sooner or later after the glittery, glamorous wedding. We can see that in the apparently 'irregular' unions of divorced and remarried couples we may find forms of commitment which extend the notion of family as consisting of the biological children of two parents living together. We have questioned an over-emphasis on the inter-personal relationship as perhaps placing an undue burden on a couple and perhaps not sufficiently recognising the network of relationships of which this union forms a part.

Life-giving relationships
My sense in relation to same sex unions is that we will not resolve that issue by giving it the goldfish bowl treatment. When such couples seek recognition, they remind us that, not only are we not isolated and solitary human beings, but that we are all called to relationship and that such relationships weave us into the larger community. To make a public commitment of love and fidelity is also to ask the community to support that love and to be faithful to it. We, too, make that solemn promise as part of the marriage ceremony. The life that is generated in the

relationship has its source in the life which has been given to it and which will in turn flow out from it. The sexual expression is then truly re-creational. This sexual energy is not confined to the procreation of children. With couples of the same sex, their life-giving love may flow out, not just to sustain one another, but also in the care of sick companions, in the care of the vulnerable elderly, in acts of friendship, in acts of creative endeavour, and in numerous other ways.

My sense is that the morality or otherwise of so-called irregular unions, be they of couples, of the same sex or of divorced and remarried couples, or of co-habiting couples, can only be judged contextually. One could ask the question, are these relationships life-giving? Is the community as a whole deprived of the possible gifts of these people by excluding them? These become different kinds of questions. They are not about looking at such relationships under the microscope as if such people were isolated from the rest of the community, but they are about seeing these situations as flowing into the wider stream of possible living in human community. They do not ask, 'what can we teach these "disordered" people?', but 'what might we learn about the human capacity for love by observing such people?' Might we learn something about the profound nature of friendship as the basis for all relationships? Might we learn something more about sexuality as the complex language of relationship? Might we learn something about difference as gift to be delighted in, and not threatened by? Might we learn something about a compassion that can suffer with the dying beloved? Might we learn about a creative love caught up into the Trinity of divine love? Equally, inclusion in the blessings of the community gives that community a say in discerning both what is good and what falls short of loving in these relationships. It would be misguided to assume that all will live 'happily ever after' if we bless those in same sex or other relationships. Such couples should not have the added stress of the burden of perfection, but should be allowed the 'doing as well as we can' which is permitted to the rest of us, who are also 'walking wounded' and fragile human beings.[7]

Making moral judgements depends not simply on the act itself but also on the context, and on the presuppositions or range of vision of the one judging. We tend to see things not as they are but as we are. We have a limited range of vision in relation to the moral issues that confront us at the beginning of this millennium. The route that I am proposing argues that we seek to learn from the re-ordering of relationships, from the re-structuring of families. We seek to be open to the possibility that families may be extended to include those who have no biological link, but who are brought together to form small human communities. Instead of condemning such arrangements, we might seek ways of enabling such groups to be sustaining and life-giving, particularly for their most vulnerable members.

The sacrament of community
I can see a great danger for same sex couples if they are taken into our failing myth of 'romantic love' which can lead simply to egoism *à deux*, or to a devastating sense of failure when the fairy-tale collapses. However, I see great hope for such couples if they are accepted into and blessed by a community which commits itself to them, and they to it, as a mutually supportive network. We need to redefine our sense of family so that it is no longer 'the little house on the prairie,' (or more likely on the estate in the gated community), but a more open structure. It is interesting to observe how such small but significant structures of mutual care can arise. I can think of one recent example. A friend spent some time in hospital. Each time I visited I became aware of the care, not simply which the nursing staff offered, though that was considerable, but rather the care which each patient offered the other. Words of encouragement were constantly spoken. 'How are you?' I would ask, 'I'm fine but X had a bad night, we're concerned about him.' The hospital ward became 'the family,' became the small community of mutual affection and support. There are many such examples of simple forms of reaching out, all of which extend the life-giving experience which should radiate from the centre of any relationship.

So, finally, I want to affirm the value of intimate loving as at the heart of human relationship – it is for this that we were created. We are not made to be autonomous and isolated persons, but we are all called to communion. As we look at the radical re-ordering of relationships in our time, we need to find ways of discerning what is good, what is life-giving, not just for the couples involved, but for the whole community. We will need to look at ways of covenanting these different forms of relationship to enable those involved to commit themselves to faithful – and if they are so graced – to life-long love.

The capacity to love is of God, of this much we are sure. How it is expressed differs from person to person, culture to culture, but where it radiates life let us reach out to it and support it, bless it and be blessed by it.

CHAPTER EIGHT

Homosexuals in the church

Raphael Gallagher CSsR

'Coming out' has a particular meaning for homosexuals. But where do you 'go' when you 'come out'? Some few go into a church. This 'coming and going' is an apt metaphor for the confused identity of homosexuals in the Catholic church.

We need to start with a metaphor, because the conceptual debate about homosexuals in the church has become polarised. The official teaching of the church is relatively clear. Having a homosexual inclination or orientation is not considered a sin, but is seen as a tendency towards an intrinsic moral evil (the performance of homosexual acts) and this is referred to as an objective disorder. This is only relatively clear, because I cannot find agreement on some of the key words such as 'inclination', 'orientation' and 'objective disorder'.

One thing is clear in the teaching however, and maybe this is where to start. Homosexual acts are immoral because they are unnatural. The moral teaching of the theological manuals, and not just recent official statements by the Vatican, presume this point. The reasoning is that the sexual instinct in all animals (including the human animal) is naturally directed towards procreation. Assumed in this reasoning is the natural superiority of the male to the female. The moral argument thus turns on acting according to our nature in our sexual lives. Apart from auto-eroticism, which was usually discussed in a different moral tract, the Catholic moral tradition considered three sins as against the nature of sex: a wrong choice about the sexual organ (anal coitus), the sexual partner (homosexuality) or sexual species (bestiality). The sinfulness was precisely in the misplaced sexual act. All sexual acts, following the venereal pleasure principle, were to be directed towards the procreation of children in a valid and stable married union between a man and a woman. Everything else was unnatural.

Does this description of the nature of homosexual activity correspond to what we now know about the nature of homosexual persons? That is the critical moral question since it involves a presumed axis of continuity between activity and identity in a person.

The analysis of this question involves a number of steps. Firstly, the indiscriminate use of the word 'homosexuality' should be avoided because there is a common confusion between homosexuals, homosexual practices, transvestites and transsexuals. These are differing realities. Grouping them together under 'homosexuality' as a generalised term leaves little room for necessary distinctions. Secondly, the term 'homosexual' should not be used in a reductionist way as if it automatically gave us all we need to know about a person's character. To tell me I am 'heterosexual' says very little about the sort of ambiguous character I might be. These two moves are necessary for etymological reasons. While the adjective 'sexual' has a long history with roots in the Latin language, the word 'sexuality' is much more recent, dating to the nineteenth century. Homosexuality, as a category used in the English language, dates to 1892, taken from the German of a few years previously. Homosexuality, being of recent origin, lacks the clarity of many neologisms. The axis of continuity between homosexual activity and homosexual identity is not only an etymological problem. It is a moral one linked to the metaphor of coming out of the closet and going into the church.

The core issue to be faced is our gender identity. Identity can be taken to mean, more or less, the sense we have of ourselves. Gender, as a grammatical term, is usually bipolar (masculine, feminine), though we should note the references of cultural anthropologists to some areas that seem to admit a third gender. It is the combination of identity and gender that is raising the interesting questions for morality. One thing is becoming clear in a discussion that, admittedly, is in its initial stages: gender identity cannot be reduced to a biological identity specified by sexual relationships. This is an added reason, more important than the etymological ones, why the indiscriminate use of the term 'homosexuality' is unhelpful. We need to move from conceptual arguments about actions to metaphorical descriptions of people.

Who is the person coming out?
When we talk about homosexuals and the church there are serious implications to be drawn from what I have said. We need to differentiate carefully between those who 'come out,' and be sensitive to where they may have come from.

The starting point is gender identification: people identify themselves as feminine or masculine. Current research has still not solved the longstanding question of whether this gender identification is a result of cultural influences or innate predispositions. I am of the view that, whether as a consequence of nature or culture, once gender identification is established it is practically irreversible. Everyone does not hold this view, but it corresponds to my experience and my study. A person who is biologically feminine (masculine) perceives himself or herself as living a different gender, a female identity trapped in a male body, or the opposite. Society, and the church, tends to treat these people as part of the phenomenon of homosexuality. On the basis of what I have already said, that is simply not the case. Miracles do happen: sex change operations can help. But there is still a major dilemma arising out of our theological tradition: activity, whether considered natural or unnatural, is not a flexible enough category to deal with the profound implications of gender identification.

Different in its typology is another group of people who come out and go in (again?) as members of the Catholic church. Some people are erotically attracted to people of their own sex: I use the word 'attraction' because the phenomenon can be a single, prevalent or dominant factor in a person's life. Attraction does not necessarily mean engagement in sexual activity. If this attraction is profound, in the sense that it is shaped during the early years (months?) of life, we are faced with a reality close to, but different from, gender identification as I explained it. Some people talk of this attraction as being scientifically reversible: the evidence does not convince me. The suffering of some people is so heartrending that they should be allowed try these medical paths. What I would definitely exclude are the types of 'cures' offered by fundamentalist groups: these offer a vengeful model of God and a simplistic view of the homosexual person as one who is to be considered as sick.

A third typology is that of people who assume, or are forced to assume, a homosexual role in society. Here we are dealing with a phenomenon outside human personal identity or attraction: the pressure comes from a social group to behave or dress as if one were homosexual. It is not uncommon for people who find themselves in roles that were not considered normal for their sex (women soldiers?) to begin to assume roles more associated with the other sex. I think this phenomenon may be more diffused in our society than we imagine, given the unisex culture that is emerging. A person may decide to continue in this role even when they move out of the social ambience where it was more or less forced on them. Abandoning the role is easy, compared to the first two typologies, provided there is a reasonable level of inner freedom involved in the choice.

There is a fourth group to be taken into consideration if my metaphor of 'coming out-moving in' is to be complete. The particular conditions in which a person is forced to live can lead to sexual behaviour not homogenous with basic attraction or deep identity: all-male, or all-female, environments are the classic examples. These are rarer now in Irish society compared to the recent past, but there are still some. Such behaviour, though brief, can affect identity and attraction, especially if it occurs at a younger age. A possible complicating factor is the difference between active and passive homosexuals. This phenomenon is usually transitory, but care is needed on this point. I have met some youngish people who feel themselves 'condemned to be gay' because there is an occasional re-emergence of a long-ago friendship. I have met others, particularly in middle age, who begin to doubt their heterosexual choices because they are disillusioned at an emotional level: maybe, they begin to think, that teenage crush was the real thing after all?

These categories are no more than sketches, and they certainly need to be studied and explained in greater depth than I have done here. My synthesis is meant to highlight a simple but crucial point in the coming-out part of my metaphor. The legacy of our Catholic theological language on homosexuality has left us ill-equipped to deal with the fact that there is a great variety in the typology of people who come out as homosexuals. This does not imply a moral relativity in terms of norms, but it certainly implies a crucial need to be sensitive to the differing circumstances in which people experience themselves as homosexuals. From where one starts, in terms of the typologies I have described, will say much about how we meet these people when they come out. Instead of taking the easy road of blaming the past theologians for their obviously out-of-date views on human nature and the too easy reduction of all sexual discourse to a minute analysis of sexual acts, we should devote our energy to the implications of these, and other, typologies. Scapegoating previous theologians can give us a smug feeling of being wiser and superior: it is of little benefit to current debates if we do not go the extra mile to engage with the knowledge that we now have and which was not available in the past.

And where is the person going into?

It is not *what* the church teaches about homosexual people and their acts that is the only difficulty. *How* the church teaches is as difficult a problem. This brings me to the second part of my metaphor: homosexual people who come into the church are struggling with their identity as Catholics. The sense of being in the church, when it is mediated only through official moral statements, is shallow ground on which to forge that identity.

Being baptised into the Catholic church is of course the

cornerstone. We are initiated into the church, washed 'in the name of the Father and of the Son and of the Holy Spirit' so that we receive a new identity. We put on Christ. It is how this cornerstone becomes the basis of the new community of being in the church that presents us with some interesting possibilities for the consideration of the adult identity of homosexual Catholics.

My thesis is that the way we celebrate liturgy, and particularly the Eucharist, is so decisive in shaping our desires and postures that it should be considered as the key moment in how the church helps homosexuals to live their Catholic identity. This identity has been given in a true but infant form in the first sacrament of initiation. I regret the poor quality of liturgical celebration in the Irish church, and I am particularly saddened when homosexuals find no nourishment for their fragile identity by their participation in these liturgies. A partial solution has been found in those homosexual groups who have an occasional liturgy or Eucharist for themselves, often inviting trusted family members and friends to participate. This is commendable, but the wider question of how liturgical celebration shapes Catholic identity should be pursued. Being a ghetto Catholic for a privileged few is a poor substitute for the rich identity that can come from wholesome liturgical celebration in the community that, obviously, includes more than homosexual members.

The first advantage will come from having the proper context within which to hear and respect church teaching. There is an analogy with the reading of holy scripture. Before we can come to an understanding of any passage of the bible, even before we begin the process of the scientific exegesis of a particular biblical quotation, we need to have a sense of the whole purpose of the bible. We don't go to the bible for historical, scientific or philosophical expositions, as these are normally understood. What we find in the scriptures is the story of the interpretation of everything – things visible and invisible, human life and universal destiny – as seen from God's point of view. Unless we grasp that, we will never get the inner sense of a particular book or passage of scripture. It is a sort of paradox: we have to know the end of the story before we can grasp the detail. I think this is analogical to how we might interpret church teaching on homosexual questions. Until we know the eschatological purpose of the foundation of the church on Christ (the end of the story, so to speak) we will not grasp the details of the teaching of the earthly church on any particular topic. My interest here is, of course, the question of homosexual Catholic identity, but I think the argument could be used in other areas as well.

The core of the church's identity, and therefore that which is most likely to influence the lifelong project of our own Christian identity, is the liturgical celebration of the Eucharist. This celebration can be seen, from one point of view, as the conscious preparation of how we are to live. It is in this sense that I mean our desires and postures are shaped by eucharistic celebration. The Eucharist is not to be judged as the remote preparation for life, still less is it to be seen as an occasion that we use to exhort people to live moral lives. The celebration of the Eucharist shapes and forms us, and in this precise sense it gives us our identity. We enter the eucharistic celebration already gifted with a basic identity through baptism: but this is a work-in-progress as we strive to become fully formed Christians.

There are four core elements within the eucharistic celebration. I will comment briefly on each of these, and then indicate how these could be productive in the struggle for Catholic identity as a homosexual.

The primary moment is thanksgiving, so much so that we can define the Eucharist simply as giving thanks. 'Blessed are you, O Lord our God': we continually name God in the various prayers of the Eucharist for the explicit reason that we know that we have been called together, in his name, for the specific purpose of giving thanks. This opens into a second moment: while we thank God for who he is, we do so through an action of remembrance: 'Do this in memory of me '. But neither thanksgiving nor memory is humanly possible, before God, unless we acknowledge our humanity. This is not a generalised sense of

'okay, I'm human like the rest of the folk here;' in the celebration of
the Eucharist we see deeply into our humanity by acknowledging
our sins. 'Lord, have mercy ... *Kyrie eleison.*' The confession of the
greatness of God, to whom we give thanks and in whose memory
we celebrate, leads us to a particular aspect of confession, that of
purposely acknowledging our sins. Because these three moments
happen in the community assembled together, it is easy to grasp
the fourth element of eucharistic celebration: intercessory prayers,
for ourselves and others. We hold the world and the ambivalence
of life, other's and ours, before God: we intercede for all that is
needed. 'Lord, hear our prayer, Lord, hear us.'

This schematic, not to say dry, presentation of the elements
of the Eucharist may seem far removed from the drama of being
a Catholic homosexual. I obviously think not. The liturgical celebration of the Eucharist is the conscious preparation for how we
live: the bringing to consciousness of the elements of thanksgiving, memory, sinfulness and intercession (particularly if it is
done on a regular basis) will surely deeply shape our desires
and postures. I am increasingly concerned that the homosexual
question as it is being debated in the church, and hotly so, is
based on a narrow moral premise. The identity of Catholics,
homosexual or not, is being driven by how they stand on this
moral question. There is so much more involved in Christian
identity than where one stands on a particular moral question. It
is to be regretted that the link between liturgy and (homosexual)
life has been narrowed to a focus on just one aspect of a complex
reality.

From morality to metaphors
The journey of coming out, for any of the typologies of homosexuals I mentioned, is a painful journey. The continuation of
this journey as a coming into the church, if it happens, is another
complex process. I have tried to hint that the reduction of both
journeys to an intellectual debate about sexual acts and moral
practices is altogether too risky. People's lives, and salvation, are
at stake.

That much-abused word 'pastoral' may be a key to under-standing my metaphorical approach. To be pastoral is not a sim-ple matter of the application of abstract principles to concrete cases. Being pastoral is the mode of how we think with, and in, the church. Homosexual people are not the objects of the pas-toral care of the church; they are independent subjects, under the rule of Christ like the rest of us. Understanding this has been the major lesson of my thirty-year experience with homosexual people. When I started in this ministry all those years ago, I made the mistake of seeing them as the objects of my pastoral concern. I thought I was doing good work, particularly as I was confident that I had all the answers, neatly pre-packaged, and delivered them with a smile. My error was a double one: seeing the homosexual as an object of my pity, and reducing this 'ob-ject' to just one aspect of a complex life, the sexual one.

Acknowledging that mistake is the way in which I think the schematic presentation of the significance of the Eucharist for forging an ongoing identity for Catholic homosexuals can be enlightening. Giving thanks to God? That is easy in the peak moments of life, but for many homosexuals it is far from easy, particularly when they see their homosexuality as an inner tor-ment or as a punishment from God. Do this in memory of me? Many homosexuals are so troubled by other memories that it is very difficult to come near a sense of being together in memory of the Lord. Not to mention those many homosexuals who will not come to the memory service because they feel they have al-ready been prejudged by the church as unworthy to be present because of their 'disorder'. Lord, have mercy? Yes, of course homosexuals are capable of acknowledging their sins, but for many it can be done in a very silent mode for fear of rejection by the community or its ministers. Lord, hear my prayer? Again, homosexual persons are very capable of praying for others, but there is quite often a particular problem. Because they are isolated or, worse, mocked and ridiculed, there is the danger that a homosexual becomes introspective and self-obsessed. This is not a good space from which to think of the needs of others.

Coming out has become easier in Ireland, even though there is still a strong homophobic element in our society. There are, at least, some oases where homosexuals are accepted. Going into the church is less easy. The resolution of the identity issues of homosexuals will be mainly in the hands of the professional researchers: I wish them well, and I hope that their research will not be driven by ideological prejudice or monetary ambition. The forming of the Catholic identity for homosexuals is more directly in the hands of people committed to the church. It is urgent that we move from the narrow categories of the present divisive debates towards a view of a eucharistic church that shapes our desires and postures. All of them, and not just the sexual ones.

Even if it is the moral implications of being a homosexual that seems to hold the most fascination, and causes the most intense divisions, it is not the only question. Many strands, particularly evident in the rich liturgical tapestry of the Eucharist, weave Catholic identity. More attention to this could be enriching, and it would place the moral question of homosexuality as one among others. The metaphor of coming out and going in has been used here with homosexual people in mind, but their Catholic identity will depend on how the rest of us also decide to shape our desires and nourish our virtues.[1]

CHAPTER NINE

Catholic fundamentalism

Gabriel Daly OSA

Anyone with even a mild interest in words must be fascinated by the seventy-year old history of the word 'fundamentalism.' How on earth could a word which was coined by a pious North American Protestant in the 1920s come to be applicable to an Iraqi suicide bomber? It is hard to think of any other word with such a dramatically developing history. This history gives us an immediate clue to what has happened. People have found within the various world religions analogies to what Curtis Lee Laws, editor of the Northern Baptist newspaper, *The Watchman Examiner*, meant when he wrote in 1920 that a 'fundamentalist' is a person willing to 'do battle royal' for the fundamentals of the faith. 'It was both a description and a call to action, and the name stuck.'[1]

In this connection it is worth reflecting briefly on a question which often arises when there is talk about 'isms.' People not unreasonably protest against labels which confine them within categories which seem to them to be unrepresentative of their real views and which leave them open to guilt by association, as it were. There is, however, also a reverse side to this coin. One sometimes comes across people who are so busy protesting against 'labels' that they simply fail to accept any responsibility for the views they actually hold, because they will not allow them to be named. Such protest amounts in the end to an assault on language and communication. This has particular relevance for the situation in the Roman Catholic Church. In attempting to describe it one needs certainly to avoid prejudiced generalisations. Nevertheless by the same token one also needs to exercise the right to try to describe it, especially if one happens to believe that it is inimical to Christian faith and witness in the modern world.

Defining fundamentalism

The central defining element in both original fundamentalism and all later derivations is a fierce opposition to modernism, understood as any attempt to bring Christianity into a mutually fruitful relationship with modern thought. There are many different types of fundamentalism, but anti-modernism (or anti-liberalism) is a constant element in all of them. Fundamentalism is always *reactive*. It is always a response to a perceived and, to some, an unacceptable liberalisation of thought.

When in the 1900s the Southern Californian oil millionaire, Lyman Stewart, was looking for an editor for what he planned as a series of paperback books which would be a 'Testimonial to the truth', he chose A. C. Dixon, a well-known evangelist whom he had heard preaching against 'one of those infidel professors' in Chicago University. The result was a series of twelve volumes published between 1910 and 1915 under the general title *The Fundamentals*. In 1920 Curtis Lee Laws proclaimed himself a 'fundamentalist,' and so the term was born.

Dixon's phrase 'infidel professor' is a key to what conservative American Protestantism was worried about. It wanted to rescue the bible from the clutches of the academics. Throughout the nineteenth century Protestant theological scholarship, especially in Germany, had attempted to respond to the challenge of the eighteenth century Enlightenment, with its emphasis on reason and experience. University theologians fought to keep their subject present and respected in academic circles. As often happens to Roman Catholic theologians today, this effort frequently made them the object of church suspicion. The French liberal Protestant, Jean Reville, argued that religious liberalism was a direct consequence of the Protestant principle of 'freedom of enquiry' and 'the religious supremacy of the individual conscience.' There is evidence that some of the fundamentalists were uneasily aware of liberal theology's claim to be more truly Protestant than their own. (This argument would of course be no help to a Catholic theologian in difficulties with the Vatican!)

In general, liberal theology transformed a conception of religious truth as infallible propositions into a system of human and relative symbols which do not compete with science. It relativised doctrinal and biblical statements by seeing them as a product of their age. It sponsored historical method and applied it to the bible, which had hitherto been taken as transcultural and eternally valid divine communication. This meant accepting the presence of error in the bible as well as disengaging the bible from the need for scientific reference. Biblical criticism accepted that the biblical account of creation, for example, could not be put on all fours with scientific treatment of the origin of the world and that the attempt to do so misunderstands the nature of religious truth and thereby endangers faith. Most of this was anathema to the fundamentalists, who saw it as palpable infidelity.

Characteristics of fundamentalism
The meaning of the word 'fundamentalism' in the 1920s is clear enough. Taking it together with the meanings it has acquired since then, one might at this point attempt a summary of the main characteristics of fundamentalism in general before enquiring into its Roman Catholic manifestation.

- Fundamentalism is always a reaction against a perceived period of liberal and relaxed standards in doctrine or morality.
- It is both a diagnosis and a call to action. It looks at the church and at the world and finds in both signs of religious and moral decomposition. As a remedy it prescribes a reaffirmation of basic or fundamental truths and courses of action.
- It is impatient with those doubts and hesitations which tend to characterise a normal thoughtful faith and it sees them as signs of a lack of faith or moral commitment. It needs an enemy and may find it in the liberals of its own tradition.
- Its lack of openness to, and respect for, views opposed to its own gives it undoubted power which can often be contrasted with the seeming vacillations and qualifications of more thoughtful and critical views.
- It tends to be hostile to the ecumenical spirit and condemns

openness to the views of others as weakness and betrayal of the truth.

- It offers certainties and securities by giving simplistic answers to complicated questions and in consequence may appeal to people who look to religion to supply the certainties which they cannot find in secular life.
- Fundamentalism is often less about *what* one believes than *the manner* in which one believes it. It has all the ostensible strength of single-mindedness and passionate intensity. (It is worth remembering that a worthy cause can be taken up in a fundamentalist manner. A cause should not be blamed for the faults of its followers.)
- It often prefers slogans to critical thought and reasoned discourse between equals. Examples from Catholic fundamentalism are: 'The church is not a democracy' and 'à la carte' Catholicism – both used with tiresome frequency as a way of countering calls to consultation and genuinely open discussion.
- It normally lacks humour and many of the qualities that make for civilisation, especially irony. In default of irony it often resorts to crude sarcasm as a weapon to attack its enemies.

Catholic fundamentalism

The origins of Catholic fundamentalism are to be found much earlier than the reaction to Vatican II which has taken place during the pontificate of John Paul II – in fact, more than a century earlier. If one of the defining characteristics of fundamentalism is a hostile response to the challenge of modernity, and another is a strong disposition to distinguish sharply between the supernatural and the natural, then the nineteenth century papacy anticipated much of what the authors of *The Fundamentals* were later to diagnose and prescribe.

The Roman authorities, who not by reasoned argument but by brute force, defeated modernism in the early years of the twentieth century, can be correctly, if analogously, described as fundamentalist. They had the same approach to the bible as

Protestant fundamentalists had, and what is more, they claimed the power to impose their fundamentalism, biblical as well as dogmatic, on the entire church. Rome's ruthless suppression of modernism took place just before *The Fundamentals* was published.

Many of the anti-modernists described themselves as 'integralists'. Integralism was the belief that Catholic orthodoxy is expressed in, and bound up with, a logically organised system of interconnected doctrines each of which goes to make up a guaranteed whole. To challenge even the smallest and most peripheral part of this system was in their eyes to endanger the whole. The similarity to biblical fundamentalism with its emphasis on inerrancy is striking.

Rome had since the 1840s managed to persuade the Catholic church that it was under insidious attack from a modernising movement intent on destroying the faith of its members. As John Kent has perceptively pointed out, the truth is that the church was in the grip of 'a vigorous anti-modernising movement which took and kept the initiative. It was not potential liberal change or socialist revolution which made the running, the church was being ruled by a counter-revolution which constantly presented itself as the victim.'[2]

Integralism and anti-modernism were still being practised up to, and even during, Vatican II. Pope John XXIII's *aggiornamento* proved fatal to the integralist system. For the next decade or so a sense of euphoria swept over a good part of the church. There was a powerful sense of liberation in the air. In the 1960s scarcely anyone noticed that this 'happy hour' would not last and that a theological hangover was fast approaching. Catholic theologians quickly discovered, and entered, the world from which officially sanctioned fundamentalism had protected them. They soon realised that freedom from official fundamentalism was freedom to be as cognitively miserable as any enlightened Protestant theologian.

Engagement with modernity

Modernity is not what it used to be. Facing up to it in the early twenty-first century is significantly different from doing so over a period of more than two centuries, as Protestant theologians have done. Protestants have received and absorbed their shocks in comparatively small doses and over an extended period. Catholics got theirs in one high tension burst, as they absorbed vast quantities of radiation from both the Reformation and the Enlightenment in less than a decade.

Roman Catholicism had postponed its inevitable engagement with modernity until the 1960s just when modernity itself was in trouble. The experience, though exhilarating, has been not unlike joining a ship in keen anticipation of an exciting voyage only to discover that the ship has been quietly corroding below the water-line and that much of the voyage will have to be spent manning the pumps. Realisation of this tends to make so much ecclesiastical activity seem like the proverbial rearranging of deck chairs on the Titanic.

The last forty years constitute a unique period in the history of the Catholic Church. These years witnessed a radical break with the past. From the start it was clear that there would be a backlash against the effects of Vatican II, if not indeed against the council itself. It remained to be seen what form it would take. To approach it from the perspective of fundamentalism is both fascinating and problematic. If one accepts that pre-conciliar mainline Roman Catholicism was in some sense institutionalised fundamentalism, then one has to ask what has actually replaced it since the council.

Paul VI fretted about all that was happening in the church, but he was too committed to the vision and achievements of the council to lead a reaction against it. The ambiguity of his papacy was, however, interrupted by one radical and far-reaching decision, when he chose to reject the advice of the body set up to advise him on marriage, sexuality and the family and opted instead for a reiteration of the ban on contraception. *Humanae Vitae* was a highly symbolic act plainly concerned more with church authority than with the substantive moral issues it dealt with. It created an instant crisis in the church marked by protests, defiance, some defections and a great deal of disillusionment. Even bishops not known for liberal thinking were taken aback and tried to soften the harsh impact of the encyclical while seeming to be of one mind with the pope.

Humanae Vitae and fundamentalist reaction
The encyclical had its enthusiastic supporters as well. An ultra rightwing North American response to *Humanae Vitae* created a significant precedent by bringing into existence a group under the title of *Catholics United for the Faith* (CUF), which has been described as 'probably the single most important conservative organisation in the United States.'[3] It makes subscription to *Humanae Vitae* the 'litmus test' of orthodoxy – something that Paul VI never tried to do but which is being done by the Vatican today. CUF sees itself as a watchdog for orthodoxy, and its members indulge in the discreditable and often malicious practice of denouncing 'liberals' to the Vatican.

Because of their obsession with authority, and knowing that they will be listened to, Catholic fundamentalists have recourse to delation (secret reporting) as one of their primary weapons. James Hitchcock, who remarks that conservative Catholics have 'bombarded the Vatican ... with complaints about the entire range of Catholic issues,' goes on to note that 'the photocopy machine and the tape recorder have proven a great boon to conservatives who have been able to send Rome copies of confidential letters, speeches, position papers, and other documents supporting their claims about "the true state of the American church".'[4] What is really regrettable is that this tale-telling is encouraged by the fact that it is never condemned as fundamentally unChristian.

Catholics United for the Faith was only the first of several Catholic fundamentalist groups to spring up in the USA and elsewhere. In 1973 a Connecticut pastor, Fr Francis Fenton, founded with strong lay support, the *Orthodox Roman Catholic*

Movement with the express intention of preserving Catholicism as it had been up to and including the pontificate of Pius XII. Fenton, who had a long-standing association with the John Birch Society, was deep into conspiracy theory, holding that the Roman Catholic Church 'is here and now in an advanced stage of *planned* destruction.'[5]

Fundamentalist schism

No reflection on Catholic fundamentalism can fail to consider Archbishop Lefebvre and his Society of St Pius X. In Lefebvre's case we are dealing with a fully schismatic movement. We are also dealing with a form of fundamentalism which had roots deep in post-Revolution French church history. Lefebvre was a monarchist and a dedicated opponent of the French Revolution and its Declaration of Human Rights. He was influenced as a student by Henri le Boch who was rector of the French College in Rome and was condemned together with Cardinal Louis Billot by Pius XI for membership of *Action Française*, an extreme right-wing political and cultural movement marked by fanatical anti-modernism and anti-semitism. It is no accident that Lefebvre's followers support Jean-Marie Le Pen today.

Lefebvre served for many years in French Equatorial Africa and retired to Rome just before Vatican II. At the council he fought every reforming measure and ended by opposing the entire council, which he saw as doing to the church what the Revolution had done to France. In fact, Lefebvre singled out three fruits of Vatican II as equivalents of the detested principles of the Revolution: *Liberté* is expressed in the conciliar Decree on Religious Freedom; *Egalité* is expressed in the conciliar teaching on collegiality; and *Fraternité* is expressed in the Decree on Ecumenism.

In 1970 Lefebvre set up a seminary in Ecône in Switzerland where he made the tridentine Latin Mass the symbolic corner-stone of his rejection of Vatican II. Though suspended by Paul VI in 1976 he carried on negotiations with the Vatican, and his movement spread, much to Rome's alarm. With the election of

John Paul II pressure on Lefebvre eased. Rome regarded his, and other right-wing movements, as a manifestation of 'excessive zeal' rather than as a danger to the faith. Everything possible was done to reconcile Lefebvre. Cardinal Ratzinger conceded most of what Lefebvre was looking for. Lefebvre appeared to agree, and the aroma of fatted calf was already scenting the air when suddenly and unaccountably he reneged. He died in 1991 and his followers continue in schism.

No such overtures have been made to people like Hans Küng, Edward Schillebeeckx, Charles Curran or Seán Fagan who not merely never went into schism, but who are trying to do their Christian thinking in the real if uncomfortable conditions of the modem world – a vocation which the authorities of their church plainly hold in considerable disesteem. As William Dinges has written, 'In the aftermath of the [Lefebvre] schism, the Vatican attitude toward traditionalists remains lenient and flexible, suggesting that it is the defiance of papal authority and juridical norms, not traditionalist views or beliefs, *per se*, that is the more important Vatican concern.'[6]

Fundamentalisms, it has been said, 'arise or come to prominence in times of crisis, actual or perceived'. Vatican II created a major crisis within the Roman Catholic church. For the generality of theologians it marked a new beginning which released them from a walled village out into the jungle of modernity where they discovered that life, however uncomfortable, was at least authentic.

Fundamentalism and Vatican II

Those who took fright at what the council had done were faced with a dilemma. If you believe to the point of obsession in the teaching church, what are you to do when it appears to have betrayed the core of your faith? The answers to that question throw light on the wider question of the nature of Catholic fundamentalism. There are two possible courses of action available to Catholics who are unhappy with the spirit of openness engendered in the church by Pope John XXIII and the council he called.

Some, like Lefebvre, quite simply reject the council as a heretical break with traditional church teaching. They see them-selves as the faithful remnant. They are commonly described as 'traditionalists'. They practise what has been called a doctrine of 'double election': Catholicism is the one true faith, and tradition-alists are the only true Catholics. They are, in short, overtly schismatic. Some traditionalists, known as 'sedevacantists,' (those who assert that no one in is charge) hold that there has been no valid pope since Pius XII. Fundamentalists, however, do not always agree with each other, and Lefebvre forbade his fol-lowers to associate with them.

The other, and by far the more common way, of dealing with the dilemma is disturbingly equivocal. Those who resort to this stratagem accept the authority of the council in theory but try to interpret it from a preconciliar perspective. This can be done in several ways. With Cardinal Ratzinger they can assert that Vatican II was 'in strictest continuity with both previous coun-cils.'[7] For those who know what Vatican II actually did, this as-sertion opens up an exceedingly wide credibility gap. Quite a large number of Catholics who would not see themselves as fun-damentalists, affirm some such continuity often without saying whether, and to what extent, they also assert a *dis*continuity be-tween Vatican II and the two previous councils. (Catholics have an inbuilt instinct for discerning and proclaiming continuities.) Another stratagem is to claim that the problems in today's church are due to 'distortions' and 'excesses' that have taken place *since the council*. Perhaps the commonest stratagem is to quote selectively from the documents of Vatican II those pas-sages and sentences which were originally included in the text in order to pacify the conservative minority at the council.

Can one properly and fairly describe all this as fundamental-ism? In the case of the traditionalists one clearly can. In the case of those who accept the validity of Vatican II but try to soften its reforming features and rein in its general openness of spirit, the matter may be less clear. Some of these subscribe to a pro-gramme of 'restoration' which enjoys a good deal of official approval and encouragement. At the very least one can say that in reacting against what is perceived as liberalism in the church and irreligion in the world, the restoration programme undoubtedly reflects some of the features of fundamentalism. It is separatist, less in a schismatic sense than in the sense that it portrays the church as an island of grace and sanity in a sea of unfaith, moral delinquency and spiritual lassitude. Its followers see themselves as an army sent into battle not only against a corrupt world but also against effete members of the church. These restorationists are gung-ho and innocent of doubt or hesitation. They advance upon their crusade armed with all the answers and untroubled by any of the questions which modern men and women ask about God, Christ, grace, sin, the church, and the meaning of life.

Fundamentalism is a frame of mind

Fundamentalism, then, in its widest sense is a frame of mind, a narrow and rigid way of doing one's thinking. It is impatient of qualification, of shading, of suggestion rather than blunt literal statement. It dislikes the sort of dialectical thinking in which one is conscious that every assertion of value needs balancing against a counter-assertion. It is usually unaware of the weighty philosophical questions raised by the process of interpretation.

The distinguished German-American Protestant theologian, Reinhold Niebuhr, recorded in his notebook for 1927 the experience of being present as a young minister at an open forum at which he was asked when he thought the Lord would return, while another person tried to get him to agree that all religion is fantasy. Reflecting on these two opposite positions, Niebuhr wrote: 'How can an age which is so devoid of poetic imagination as ours be truly religious?' Interestingly, a year earlier, Paul Claudel, reflecting on the situation in the eighteenth and nineteenth centuries, had written: 'The crisis ... was not primarily an intellectual crisis ... I would prefer to say it was the tragedy of a starved imagination.' Niebuhr then went on to say: 'Fundamentalists have at least one characteristic in common with most scientists. Neither can understand that poetic and religious imagination has a way of arriving at truth by giving a clue to the total meaning of things without being in any sense an analytic description of detailed facts.'

Conclusion

In the end it is all largely a matter of imagination and what in the eighteenth century was called 'sensibility'. Fundamentalists seek a clarity in excess of the facts. As Maurice Blondel said about his scholastic opponents, 'They see too clearly to see properly.' They have neither the imagination nor a system of interpretation which would allow them to appreciate the poetic and metaphorical character of religious language. They do not see the value of multi-layered meaning of the kind that does not force us to choose between one layer and the others. They believe that pluralism is destructive of orthodoxy. They call for fatwahs, censorship and sackings or exclusions from teaching or executive posts. If you accused them of malice, they would shake their heads sadly at your lack of comprehension. They bluster and bully and set themselves up as guardians of orthodoxy. The gospel faces us with the difficult task of loving them - while standing up to them.

CHAPTER TEN

Law, justice and morality

Bernard Treacy OP

Discussion of the lines of intersection between law, justice and morality can take many diverse forms. It can range from an account of St Paul's teaching in the letters to the Romans and to the Galatians, to an analysis of what may have been at stake in Irish referendums of the 1980s and 1990s on the right to life of the unborn. Along the way, it can take a look at natural law thinking, and at the rediscovery of virtue ethics. Discussion of the interplay between law and morality will, inevitably, touch on many topics.

The scriptural teaching that, for the Christian, salvation consists in the free living out of the implications of accepting a graced way of life as offered by Christ rather than in adherence to legal rules, however divinely sanctioned, may seem, too often, to be ignored in practice. But it remains a subversive memory with deep and lasting power to offer renewal and new vitality. A return to scriptural insights helped lift Catholic moral thinking from being law-based and scruples-inducing. Though there are voices that speak of developments during, and since Vatican II, as opening the door to relativism, it is clear that the move away from a tradition of moral teaching based on obedience to rules and regulations has been beneficial. Beneficial in many ways, especially in moving the focus of moral teaching towards helping people to grow in moral understanding and to develop lives of virtue.

Duty to obey civil law

It is important to notice that, even in his Letter to the Romans, Paul taught that there is an obligation to submit to civil authority and to pay taxes (Rom 13:1, 6-7). By implication, this would suggest that he believed that civil law obliged the conscience of the citizen. The next generation of Christian teachers and leaders went even further in advocating obedience not just to legal rules, but also to accepted codes of household behaviour, as we see in Colossians and in the pastoral epistles.

The Christian tradition sees the moral obligation to obey law as flowing from a vision of all law as being founded on God's law. This proves itself true in so far as the laws which human beings may enact are actually focused on bringing about the common good of society. In the centuries after the conversion of Constantine the emergence of an almost theocratic Christendom, in which moral law and civil law tended to be intertwined, obscured the truth that civil law has its own distinctive purpose. In the centuries of imperial persecution and of the martyrs it was not so. Christians saw a clear distinction between the law and their Christian conscience, and were willing to act on the belief that a higher value, such as witness to the faith, could authorise them to refuse to obey a legal command. In taking the stance they did, many of the martyrs put forward a surprisingly modern view of the duty of the citizen to the state. As we find in the second century *Letter of Diognetus*, they did not see themselves as rebels against public order, even when they refused to give their loyalty to the emperor as a religious obligation.

Although Christian Europe, with its theory of the divine right of kings, tended in practice, if not in theory, to conflate divine, moral and civil law, there always were teachers who saw things differently. One might point to Thomas Aquinas, who recognised that human law can have but limited aims and cannot be expected to provide for every aspect of human living.

Conscientious objection
Stories of principled refusal to obey a law, because of commitment to a higher value, are both inspiring and rare since the age of the martyrs. Such dilemmas arose again for Christians of all traditions during the conflicts engendered by the Reformation.

If, in the western church, we consign those battles to sincere repentance for past wrong-doing and a commitment to healing the
wounds of that era, could we now begin to recognise and honour the Christian witness given by all the martyrs? Despite their
differences on church policies, Hugh Latimer and Thomas
Cranmer, as much as Edmund Campion and Thomas More,
gave their lives for the gospel and for their commitment to
Christ. Just as the Sant'Egidio Community celebrates the martyrs of the twentieth century without distinguishing between
Roman or Orthodox, Anglican or Protestant, could not a like
mutual recognition be extended to the martyrs of the sixteenth
century?

Closer to our own time, the witness of those whose insistence
on refusing military service led, in the early decades of the twentieth century, to the recognition of conscientious objection as a
category, can be mentioned. Even more awesomely inspiring is
the story of Franz Jägerstatter. This Austrian farmer refused his
call-up to Hitler's army not as a conscientious objector, but because he believed the war Hitler was engaging in was unjust. No
amount of advice from clergy or entreaty from his family could
shift him from his conscientious position. He accepted the death
penalty rather than conform to an unjust law. His witness was
heart-breaking in its starkness.

Others have followed the principle that laws are not of obligation if they offend against a moral principle, by such actions as
withholding that portion of their tax bill which relates, for example, to military budgets. However valuable as an act of witness,
this type of action is likely to be ultimately forlorn as modern
governments have such inexorable tax-collection systems.

Before leaving the topic of giving adherence to a higher
moral value at the expense of obeying the law of the land, it
would be interesting to know whether any lawyer in Ireland or
Britain in the past (or today in the United States) declined appointment to the bench because of a conscientious objection to
the possibility of having to pass a death sentence.

Ethical values are a base for laws

If there are moral values that can, on occasion, prompt a citizen to choose them rather than obey the law, this is not to say that the law is devoid of moral content. Many branches of law are firmly based on ethical values. Some examples may be cited. When a state's Constitution guarantees to uphold the fundamental personal rights of its citizens, as Bunreacht na hÉireann does in articles 40 to 44, it is enunciating a vision of human dignity – and taking active steps to make that vision a reality. The law of contract tries to ensure that there will be honesty and fairness in business dealings; at times it even tries to curtail that advantage which a large business corporation can obtain over the individual customer. The law of negligence is directed towards ensuring that people accept responsibility for the consequences of their actions. One of the functions of criminal law is to protect the life, health and property of citizens by punishing those who offend against any of these rights.

But the primary function of a legal system is to promote the common good of society, by providing structures which enable citizens to co-operate, to be governed and to build up a community in which justice may flourish. Some of the laws enacted for these purposes may have ethical aims in view, such as laws punishing acts of killing, maiming or theft. Other laws may be more directed towards ensuring harmonious conduct. Whether traffic travels on the left or on the right hand side of the road is of no moral significance in itself. That all road-users would travel in such a way as puts neither themselves nor others in danger is manifestly for the common good, and laws designed to ensure mutual safety among road-users can acquire a moral imperative because of the ethical requirement to take responsibility for one's actions.

If obedience to legal rules is a moral obligation, does it follow that the law can change moral perceptions and commitments? People would not immerse themselves in campaigns for legal changes which incorporate moral insights if they did not believe that a change in people's attitudes would follow. Experience would seem to confirm this assumption. The Succession Act (1965), by changing the rules on inheritance so that it became impossible for a spouse to exclude the survivor from inheriting, brought a much needed element of equality into family life. The Unfair Dismissals Act (1977) introduced a welcome balance of rights into the workplace. Legislation of recent years which outlaws discrimination, whether the grounds that give rise to it be ethnic, religious, or racial, is designed to enable people to overcome prejudice.

Whether people actually act morally when obeying legal rules is difficult to assess. A person may implement equality procedures or be meticulous in meeting tax obligations, but do so with such an air of resentment that the moral value of compliance with the law is vitiated. On the other hand, what might begin as a reluctant compliance with newly imposed legal obligations may grow into an understanding of the moral value at stake and, eventually, into a wholehearted acceptance of that value. This may well be happening in respect of laws banning drink driving or speeding on the roads. In such ways, the law can function as a pedagogue, drawing people into commitment to moral values they might not otherwise accept.

Law and moral values
Law can often open one's eyes to the presence of evil in the world. St Paul's comment that 'through the law comes knowledge of sin' (Rom 3:20) will make sense to anyone who studies commercial law. Students learn of ways of being dishonest and/or gaining an unfair advantage over others which might not otherwise occur to them. This comes from studying statutes or court decisions which close off access to ingenious devices for manipulating business unjustly or unfairly. Law must be constantly vigilant.

Discussion of what moral values may appropriately be enshrined in law did not start with the referendum debates on the right to life for the unborn, though the campaigns of the 1980s and 1990s brought the topic to the attention of the public in a

particularly intense way. Not every form of moral wrong-doing
is subjected to the sanction of the criminal law. Adultery, for example, is not a crime, though it may be invoked in seeking a separation order or a divorce. The debate on enforcing moral values
through legal sanctions exposes the distinction between positivist and natural law theories of law. The positivist approach
tends to stress that legal rules acquire their binding force simply
from the fact that they are enacted by a properly appointed leg-
islator: moral criteria are not relevant in assessing them. Thus,
under a purely positivist view, the call-up papers issued to
Franz Jägerstatter would have imposed an absolute obligation
which he should have accepted. Interestingly, the Nuremberg
tribunal which tried, convicted and passed sentence on those
principally responsible for the Nazi terror, rejecting the defence
that they were only following orders, could do so only by moving away from a purely positivist approach. As A. P. d'Entrèves
pointed out in *Natural Law*,[1] the statement that the trials were 'a
question of justice' involved stepping beyond the limits of purely
positivist thinking.

When one asks whether it is the business of the law to enforce morality as such, the famous debate of the 1960s between
Professor H. L. A. Hart and Lord Devlin set out what is at stake.[2]
This debate was sparked by a public lecture on 'The Enforcement
of Morals' delivered by Mr Justice (as he then was) Devlin, in
1959. To rehearse all the details of the debate – found in their
books *Law, liberty and morality*[3] and *The Enforcement of morals*[4] –
would be excessive in this context, but certain elements of their
arguments are worth attention. One is Professor Hart's reminder that most cases of legal enforcement of moral values in-
voke the criminal law, and thus the punishment of offenders.
For him, punishments such as deprivation of liberty or of
association with family or friends are all matters that are normally regarded as evil. Thus, if they are to be inflicted without
attracting moral condemnation, there must be a clear and accepted justification for doing so. Mr Justice Devlin summed up
his thinking by pointing out that 'a man who concedes that

morality is necessary to society must support the use of those instruments without which morality cannot be maintained.' He went on:

> The two instruments are those of teaching, which is doctrine, and of enforcement, which is the law. If morals could be taught simply on the basis that they are necessary to society, there would be no need for religion; it could be left as a purely personal affair. But morality cannot be taught in that way. Loyalty is not taught in that way either. No society has yet solved the problem of how to teach morality without religion. So the law must base itself on Christian morals and to the limit of its ability enforce them, not simply because they are the morals of most of us, nor simply because they are morals which are taught by the established church – on these points the law recognises the right to dissent – but for the compelling reason that without the help of Christian teaching the law will fail.[5]

It is clear that Devlin's central concern is to maintain the 'integrity of society'; but his thinking also recognises the need to allow as wide a compass as possible for personal freedom. For Hart, on the other hand, the task, above all, is to protect the freedom of the individual.

Freedom is indivisible
Protection of society and protection of personal freedom, these are the twin aims of any move to enforce morals through the legal system. How to reconcile these two values in any particular case will always involve difficult judgements, about which citizens may well differ in good faith. Catholic legislators or citizens may disapprove of what other citizens do with their freedom. However, that is no reason to deprive them of that freedom: freedom is indivisible, and to ensure the freedom of one group is to ensure the freedom of all groups in society, even of those who use freedom to act in ways which the believer identifies as sinful. John Courtney Murray, whose thinking underpins the Vatican II *Declaration on Religious Freedom,* eloquently

summed up the need to be wary of curtailing the freedom of the citizen, even in pursuit of a moral purpose:

> Law seeks to establish and maintain only that minimum of actualised morality that is necessary for the healthy function of the social order. It does not look to what is morally desirable, or attempt to remove every moral taint from the atmosphere of society. It enforces only what is minimally acceptable, and in this sense socially necessary.[6]

This line of thinking does not offer the kind of definite, clear-cut guidance which legislators, or citizens at large, when acting as legislators in a referendum vote, may sometimes crave. But it provides a valuable service in that it endorses their responsibility to weigh up all aspects of each question, carefully and conscientiously. When there are calls for changes in the law to provide recognition of the rights of minorities, there is need for precise and focused thinking. The simple fact of being a minority is not, of itself, a reason for recognition. People who rob banks are a minority within most societies; but no one would accept that they should be granted recognition and the right to practise their preferred choice of lifestyle.

One classical way of resolving how to accommodate questions of the legal enforcement of moral values, or questions concerning claims for minority rights, is to look to the common good of society. The word 'common' in this phrase deserves attention. It should not be read in opposition to 'individual' or 'personal'. If we look at the account of the common good given in the Vatican II document, *Constitution on the Church in the Modern World*, we see that the concept points to the need to promote personal rights as truly as it concerns social values. The Council saw the common good as 'the sum total of social conditions which enable people, either as groups or as individuals, to reach their fulfilment more fully or more easily.' (n 26)[7]

Deciding how a particular proposal fits among this 'sum total of social conditions' and whether it will actually enable people 'to reach their fulfilment' will often involve debate and discussion. The churches, through their members, their various constituent parts, and their leaders, can properly have a part in this debate. Over the centuries, church members acting out of religious conviction have contributed significantly to the development of human rights. To take only two examples, there is the work (theological and legal) of Bartolomé de las Casas in regard to the rights of native peoples, or of Francisco Vitoria in developing an ethic of just conduct in war. Here in Ireland in recent years, church bodies such as the Irish Bishops' Commission for Prisoners Overseas and the Justice Commission of the Conference of Religious of Ireland have contributed enormously to raising consciousness about the most vulnerable in society, about their rights, and about the need to mobilise resources – of resolve as much as of finance – in their defence. When church bodies step forward to contribute to discussions on the common good, they do not come empty-minded or empty-handed.

Church's place in assessment of common good
But when church bodies come into a forum which assesses the common good of society, they come on the same terms as all others taking part in the discussion. The church has no special claim to be heard, and its voice will be only as strong as its arguments are cogent. As a partner in the discussion, it will be required to listen attentively, something church bodies are not always ready to do: the remark, made not without justification, that the church is wired to transmit rather than to receive, is attributed to both Fergal O'Connor and Gabriel Daly. Sadly, if such an attitude persists, it will seriously endanger the capacity of the church to contribute helpfully in public debate. To be effective in discussions about the common good and about whether particular proposals contribute to the well-being of society, the church needs to do more than articulate its own views and listen to the views of others, valuable though these processes are. It also needs to be prepared to change its stance in order to incorporate insights articulated by others and which might not have been given sufficient weight in church statements. This would not be a matter of abandoning an essential teaching, but of being open to taking on board truthful insights wherever they come

from. The example set by Sinn Féin and the Democratic Unionist Party, of relentless repetition of a party line in tones which portray everyone else as unreasonable, is not one to follow.

When the church becomes a dialogue partner within society's discussions of the common good, it must be aware that it is thereby making itself open to scrutiny on its own record. In any discussion of justice matters, the Catholic Church is vulnerable in at least two areas. These concern the rights of members of the church. The Code of Canon Law contains many declarations of the rights of the 'members of Christ's faithful', but in the twenty-two years since the new Code was promulgated we have put no mechanisms in place to vindicate those rights. If the right 'to manifest to the sacred Pastors their views on matters which concern the good of the church' (canon 212.3) were taken seriously – as it should be, if it is a right – we would have councils and synods in every parish and diocese, and lay representatives present as of right at Synods in the Vatican.

The second moment of vulnerability concerns the procedures in place at the Congregation for the Doctrine of the Faith for investigating complaints against the teaching of theologians. The highly respected canonist Ladislas Örsy SJ has shown that the Congregation's new procedures adopted in June 1997, offend against all the principles of fair procedure held as axiomatic by modern, secular jurisprudence. In his article 'Are Church Investigation Procedures Really Just?' (*Doctrine & Life,* October 1998)[8] he compared the CDF procedures with principles such as the precise definition of offences; the separation of roles between judge and prosecutor; the right of both sides to present their case; the presumption of innocence; justice must not just be done, but must be seen to be done; there must be an opportunity for an appeal; there must be no automatic punishment. In all cases the Vatican procedures were demonstrated to fall short of what is taken as normative for fair procedure in civilised countries, in many cases failing completely. The pity of it is that the church was not always thus. In 1215, the Fourth Council of the Lateran decreed:

He who is the object of an enquiry should be present at the process and, unless absent through contumacy, should have the various headings of the enquiry explained to him, so as to allow him to defend himself; as well, he is to be informed not only of what the various witnesses have accused him of but also of the names of those witnesses.

There is a further way in which the church's reputation as a promoter of justice is besmirched by its own conduct, an aspect of church life which is likely to be much more obvious to most readers than the examples just cited. Court cases and investigations and protests concerning child sexual abuse, by some from among the clergy and members of religious orders, reveal a failure to have regard for the rights of others that is very difficult to understand. It should be a fundamental of church policy that all members have the right to receive ministry that is safe and that respects their personal integrity. Yet now we know of a long hidden scandal of clergy who used their position of trust to prey on children and on families. We know of a cardinal archbishop who had long disregarded the problem even when it was clearly presented to him, and who resigned his See only when the clergy protested at his staying on. The agony of the families concerned had not prompted Cardinal Law to take responsibility for his moving clergy whom he knew to have offended against children to positions where they could continue their abuse. Although the cardinal was given an honorary position in Rome rather than retiring completely from all offices – for obvious reasons, a source of shock and dismay for many – there are, elsewhere, welcome and unmistakable signs that the problem is now being robustly addressed.

Past tolerance of infringements of the rights of children, and the presence within the church of defective procedures such as those followed by the CDF, can give the impression that the only upholder of liberal values is the modern secular state. This view is bolstered by an assumption about the process by which the modern state emerged from the wars of religion of the sixteenth and seventeenth centuries. In this view the state proved to be the honest broker between competing religious worldviews. But another view of the origin of the modern liberal state is possible. In *Theopolitical imagination*[9] William T. Cavanaugh of St Thomas University, St Paul, argues that it is more accurate to see the wars of religion as occasions when political powers hijacked religious controversy to justify their own military adventures and the consolidation of their own power within national borders.

If we take such a view on board, there is further support for the church having the confidence to enter into public debate about the direction society should take and about those values which should be publicly endorsed and enforced as contributing to the common good. In entering such debates church bodies may find themselves treated both as allies and as being under suspicion, if an article by the influential New York-based organisation, Human Rights Watch, in *World report 2005*, indicates what may be expected in the future. The authors of 'Religion and the human rights movement', Jean-Paul Marthoz and Joseph Saunders, acknowledge that in many countries 'religion was the prime mover behind campaigns for human rights', and point out that '[i]n the 1970s and 1980s, religious and human rights groups shared many objectives, reflecting a common conviction of the universality of the human rights message and its grounding in the traditions of most religions, philosophies and civilisations.' Alongside this acknowledgement, the article is mostly a catalogue of ways in which what it terms a 'religious "blowback"' is proving a threat to human rights: a catalogue not confined to activities which could accurately be labelled 'fundamentalist'. While resisting the opposition by some religious groups to the rights of free speech, the authors recognise clearly that there 'is still space for convergence and coalitions between human rights and religious communities.'[10]

In venturing to enter that space, the church need not be at a loss over against any other participant in the debate. Neither need it stand shy before the liberal values of the modern state. The church has its own mandate to live and celebrate and speak the truth, and it should be faithful to that mandate in its life and its teaching.

Whenever it comes to take part in public discussion on justice or on legislative questions, the church must remember to come 'with clean hands', to adopt a phrase used in some branches of law. If it proclaims rights for its own members but fails to provide means of enforcing them, and if it persists in allowing its investigative procedures to be defective, it cannot but damage its own witness to justice. When the church contributes to discussions about law, justice and morality, it comes with a rich inheritance from which to draw. Taking part in such discussions is also an opportunity to examine its own record and to ensure that it is itself a haven of justice and fair process.

CHAPTER ELEVEN

Conscience and decision-making

Amelia Fleming

Many members of our increasingly secular and pluralist society question the role of the Roman Catholic understanding of the mature moral conscience. They believe a morally good life can be led without obedience to church teaching, as morality is not a Christian construct; it is a basic human reality rooted in the reason and experience of the community as a whole. A morally upright life is usually understood as a life lived in right relationship with our neighbours and our world around us, so that we can become who God wants us to be. We are all familiar with the reasonable call to give each their due, to be fair, and the concomitant need and expectation to be treated fairly. The media have copious moral statements about acts of racism, inequality, reproductive techniques and the need for honesty in all aspects of society. However, being moral should not be thought of as being only about isolated human acts, but as being part of a future-oriented growth process. The art of being in just and loving relationships involves our striving to become the persons we ought to be, and our decisions and our actions depend on who we are. Morality should also be understood in terms of intention and a fundamental disposition toward the good or toward the bad.

Approaching morality in this way, one could question the divine and ecclesial reference for the Christian conscience. This reference is necessary because our behaviour expresses our human character, and the inevitable influence of the moral principles, values, and ideals for right living of those around us in our community. In the Christian community, our moral context is based in the example of Christ, and shaped by the Christian

Trinitarian vision interpreted and handed on by the church. The first basis of any Christian moral life is the acceptance of God as superior lawgiver. The Christian moral tradition relates our belief in Christ to the sort of persons we ought to be as images of God, and the decisions we ought to make throughout our lives. We make these decisions with a certain degree of autonomy, as we are set apart from the rest of creation by virtue of our reason and free will. When we choose a course of action, we act freely according to experience and our knowledge of the difference between right and wrong, good and evil, and the understanding that we ought to do what is morally right. This awareness resides in the conscience, and for the Christian, our conscience is sometimes confusingly referred to as the voice of God within our hearts.

Is conscience the voice of God?
This notion of conscience as the voice of God was the basis of John Henry Newman's argument for the existence of God, viewed as a sense of duty, obeying the natural law to do good and avoid evil. Through the conscience, as the *Catechism* (n 1706) puts it: a law is made apparent which 'everyone is obliged to follow'. The presence of this law implies a presence of a divine lawgiver and a command implies a superior. For Newman in *The Grammar of assent*, to go against the voice of conscience results in fear and shame, implying that there is One to whom we are responsible, before whom we feel ashamed, whose claims upon us we fear.

When using the Christian metaphor of the divine voice, it is important to distinguish between the role of the moral conscience and the role of the Freudian superego in moral decision-making. This is important as God's voice could be mistaken for the human voice of church authority acting as a superego upon our decision-making. The psychological notion of the superego functions as a static regulator of behaviour in the young and the morally immature. The superego does not develop, learn or grow as the conscience does. One can see clear examples of an

active superego in children who do the 'right thing' purely out
of fear of punishment or the withdrawal of love. However, as
their personality develops and matures, they integrate and per-
sonalise parental and societal attitudes and begin to differentiate
between right and wrong for themselves. Instead of their superego commanding or forbidding behaviour, there is now a
process of intellectual reflection and judgement upon the right-
ness or wrongness of an act being done, about to be done, or already done. The expectation of reward or pleasure or the avoid-
ance of punishment are no longer motivations for right action.
The virtue or value at stake becomes motivation in itself. The
mature conscience will either command or forbid the action, and
the person is bound to act according to that conscience. Guilt remains an integral part of the correct functioning and growth of a
healthy and mature conscience. However, the manner in which
it operates differs. Instead of focusing on the past wrong action,
this moral guilt should be dynamic and future-oriented, and
used to improve one's future life and moral behaviour. It is the
continuing task of the adult to move away from legalistic, disciplinary superego responses towards the dynamism and freedom of conscience.

Conscience and authority

Prior to the belated though rapid secularisation of Irish society,
the overreaching influence in Ireland's predominantly rural
daily life was a legalistic and disciplinary Roman Church and
her teachings, with little influence from other quarters. One had
authoritative clerical figures in the primary and secondary classroom, in the parish, and in the state. The post-colonial Irish
Republic held fast to this church and its authority, identifying
nationality with religion and its behavioural regulations. The result was that we behaved according to the rules, often overriding our best instincts. More often than not, our state laws were
also church laws. However, with the advent of the secular
agents of feminism, urbanisation, and a pervasive media culture, Ireland began to remove these religious structures from

everyday private and political life. People began to think for themselves and, with a new-found confidence in their own reason and experience, are now living in the increasingly liberal, secular and affluent society of the European Union. One could argue that the individual Irish Roman Catholic began to reform his/her religious worldview by beginning to question the role and authority of the church in their lives, especially in their private lives. Some Irish Roman Catholics are now more comfortable with the Protestant worldview and its approach to ecclesial authority, and to married and female clergy. With a growing rate of inter-church marriages, Irish society is now provided with a welcome integration between denominations and opportunities for ecumenical dialogue at the domestic and cultural level.

This new breed of moderate Irish Roman Catholic opinion is dissatisfied with the overly-parental attitude to be found in some answers from the church, which tell the faithful what they should do in a given situation simply 'because we tell you so'. The issue of conscience is important in the field of contemporary moral theology, and especially within the context of the authority found in the moral teaching of the magisterium of the church. The question often raised in this regard is, in what way does conscience function in combination with authoritative teaching? Is the true liberty which should be afforded conscience hindered by continual reference to magisterial teaching? The teaching contained in the Second Vatican Council's *Gaudium et Spes*, the document on the church in the modern world, highlighted the link between freedom and the role of conscience, stressing the importance that humanity should act freely from within and not by blind impulses or by mere external constraint.

This tension between conscience and authority, be it ecclesial or state, is ancient, as dramatically illustrated in Sophocles' *Antigone*, written in fifth century Athens. The grieving Antigone is a typical Sophoclean heroine, an individual set apart by an unswerving adherence to a single principle, disregarding the cost – her life – to herself. Her purpose in attempting to give her brother an honourable burial in defiance of the king's orders was to illustrate how a law must not violate morality. Another well-known example of conscience conflicting with authority can be found in Robert Bolt's *A Man for all seasons*, where the historical layman Sir Thomas More must choose between losing his life or acting against his conscience. The politico-theological background to the play was the wish of King Henry VIII to have his marriage to his brother's widow, Catherine of Aragon, annulled by Pope Clement VII, on the grounds that it contravened the Christian law which forbade such a marriage. (This law had been dispensed by the pope at the request of both Spain and England to allow the marriage to proceed in the first place.) When Catherine could not provide a male heir to the throne, Henry then wished to marry Anne Boleyn as they were confident of her fertility. If More had been willing to give his approval to the king's second marriage, his life would have been spared, but such was his strength of conscience, he could not invite God to act as a witness to the lie. In 2002, when presenting St Thomas More to Catholic parliamentarians as their patron, Pope John Paul II, in his homily, pointed out that More never compromised his conscience, even to the point of making the supreme sacrifice so as not to disregard its voice, believing that when statesmen forsake their personal consciences for the sake of public duty, they lead their country to chaos.

Sanctity of conscience
The Second Vatican Council has attested to the inviolability of conscience in *Dignitatis Humanae* (n 3 and n 14), declaring that one should not be forced to act in a manner contrary to one's conscience. Nor, on the other hand, is one to be restrained from acting in accordance with conscience. But, when informing one's conscience, the Christian ought carefully to attend to the sacred and certain doctrine of the church.

The conflict between conscience and authority erupted in ecclesial circles with the promulgation of Pope Paul VI's encyclical *Humanae Vitae* in 1968, and continues to bubble beneath the surface with concerns regarding Pope John Paul II's 1994 Apostolic

Letter *Ordinatio Sacerdotalis* and his 1998 motu proprio *Ad Tuendam Fidem*. In recent years, this Apostolic Letter has pushed the issue of the types of obedience owed to the teachings of the magisterium to the fore in theological debate. The binding force of *Ordinatio Sacerdotalis* seems unclear. It declares that the church has no authority to ordain women to the priesthood. This Letter seems to be a response by the Roman Church to circumstances playing out within the Anglican Church. The Anglican Bishop of Bristol had ordained thirty two women on 23 March, two months prior to the promulgation of *Ordinatio Sacerdotalis*, and pressure was growing within the Roman Catholic Church itself to allow the ordination of women.

Throughout *Ordinatio Sacerdotalis*, traditional church teaching is cited and repeated, as this traditional teaching is one of the basic reasons behind the declared inability of the church to ordain women. This teaching on the non-ordination of women is 'definitively to be held' by the faithful, based on sacred scripture as proof of God's plan for his church, and the 'constant tradition' of the church. 'Constant tradition' means those teachings that have been believed everywhere, always, and by everyone. Problems have arisen with regard to the assent due to this teaching. Once again, Newman's voice echoes into our own time. He, too, is critical of this principle quoted from St Vincent of Lerins, rightly pointing out that it is not of mathematical or demonstrative character, but moral, and requires practical judgement and good sense to apply it. For instance, he wonders what is meant by 'taught *always*'? Does it mean in every century, or every year, or every month? Does 'everywhere' mean in every country, or in every diocese? Are we required to produce the direct testimony of every bishop? How many bishops, how many places, how many instances constitute a fulfilment of the test proposed? 'It is, then, from the nature of the case, a condition which can never be satisfied as fully as it might have been. It admits of various and unequal application in various instances '[1]

If the doctrine is 'definitively to be held,' infallibility is implied, yet canon law states that unless a doctrine is *clearly* established as having been infallibly defined, it is not to be under-stood as infallible. Many theologians believe that the infallibility of the teaching contained in *Ordinatio Sacerdotalis* is not clearly established, as it was not explicitly stated *ex cathedra* by John Paul II. In the official clarification, *Responsio ad Dubium*, issued on 18 November 1995 by the Congregation for the Doctrine of the Faith, responding to the doubts expressed as to the doctrinal weight of *Ordinatio Sacerdotalis*, the Congregation declared it to be the intention of the pontiff to speak infallibly on this matter. It was declared that this doctrine had already been infallibly taught by the ordinary and universal magisterium, *ubique, sem-per, et ab omnibus* (everywhere, always and by everyone). As this document was papally approved for publication, it would seem that this was indeed the case. In fact, however, this clarification did not retrospectively confer this infallibility unto the Apostolic Letter, as the pope cannot communicate his infallibility through a curial congregation.

Ad Tuendam Fidem
The *Responsio* of the Congregation did little to assuage the con-cerns expressed in theological circles regarding the assent due to this canonically uncertain infallibility. The additions and modi-fications made in Pope John Paul II's 1998 *Ad Tuendam Fidem* (to protect the faith) were made in order to underline and give canonical status to the type of assent required when dealing with definitive, but non-infallible, church teachings such as that contained in *Ordinatio Sacerdotalis*. In *Ad Tuendam Fidem*, Pope John Paul II amended the Code of Canon Law. The first change deals with canon 750, which concerns doctrines which are ir-reformable and which require the assent of theological faith by all members of the faithful. The proposition of an irreformable doctrine can never be rejected as wrong, although the statement or wording may be expressed differently for a new historical context. These are doctrines divinely revealed, such as the arti-cles of the Creed, the Christological and the Marian dogmas. He also added a new text concerned with truths 'definitively to be

held' concerning faith and morals which are necessarily connected with revelation because of a historical relationship or logical connection. Cardinal Ratzinger emphasises in the *Explanatory
Note* which accompanied *Ad Tuendam Fidem* (though not specifically linked to it) that there is no difference between the nature of
the assent required by truths divinely revealed and those 'definitively to be held'. Examples given by Cardinal Ratzinger in §11
of the commentary include the church's teaching on euthanasia,
and the ruling out of any possibility of ordaining women to the
priesthood. The latter example could hardly have been omitted
as it had been proclaimed by the pope as requiring 'definitive'
assent in *Ordinatio Sacerdotalis* (n 4).

There is now confusion about the distinction between infallible and non-infallible teachings by the use of the adjective 'definitive.' Many theologians believe that the Holy Spirit works
through every member of the faithful, therefore, in assisting the
magisterium in its reformable teachings preserving the church
from defect, the Spirit may also be working through dialogue
and dissent to correct a teaching that remains reformable. Some
theologians are of the opinion that it is impossible for the Holy
Spirit to allow the church to give erroneous moral guidance, but
even a casual reading of ecclesiastical history shows that the
church has been wrong in the past, and there is no *a priori* reason
to say that it could not be wrong in some of its current teaching.
It is, therefore, highly regrettable that all discussion on the possible ordination of women has been banned. It is only through debate and discussion that the truth can be reached, 'for the human
mind has a natural thirst for truth and will only rest when convinced by truth. A teacher may help in the search, but no good
teacher would command that seekers stop thinking and search-
ing.'[2] The rights of Catholics to discuss religious matters are included in *Gaudium et Spes* (n 62), and in the 1983 Code of Canon
Law (212.3) and yet often theologians and others are forbidden
to write or dialogue on a question which the Vatican believes is
settled. Papal authority and power is now used to block theological debate on women's ordination. Trying to inform and educ-

ate the conscience of the people of God without open, public and
in-house discussion makes it difficult to reach the truth.

'To conscience first, to the pope afterwards!'
Newman, both as an Anglican and as a Roman Catholic, considered the possibility of such conflict between conscience and authority. When discussing Newman's theology of conscience, the
oft-quoted after-dinner toast in his *Letter to the Duke of Norfolk* is
immediately brought to mind. 'Certainly, if I am obliged to
bring religion into after-dinner toasts, (which indeed does not
seem quite the thing) I shall drink – to the pope, if you please –
still, to conscience first, and to the pope afterwards.'

Newman's after-dinner toast is often mistakenly used to
imply that Newman is an advocate of an indulgent use of the
concept of the liberty of conscience over the authority of any
church teaching. This toast has been misunderstood as it is so
often quoted out of context. Newman's toast is placed at the end
of his chapter on conscience, and refers to a pope giving particular orders, in particular situations – an area in which he does not
enjoy the charism of infallibility. Newman, giving examples of
such instances when an individual conscience as a practical dictate may collide with a papal injunction, speaks of hypothetical
papal orders for clerical teetotalism and mandatory lotteries in
aid of the missions. In these cases, should one's conscience object to such orders, one is obliged to follow it. In his Anglican
sermons, stressing the need for one to follow one's conscience,
Newman spoke of his conviction that the truly conscientious
person could not anger God. As a Catholic, Newman discussed
this conviction on the supremacy of individual conscience in the
Letter to the Duke of Norfolk, speaking of the inviolability and dignity of conscience, recognising conscience in the divine law as
the rule of ethical truth, the standard of right and wrong. In this
he anticipated the shift to the person-centred moral teaching of
the Second Vatican Council in *Gaudium et Spes*. However, the
Second Vatican Council did not take its teaching on conscience
from Newman specifically. The Council's passage on conscience

can be traced to well over a hundred sources, excluding Newman for, as admitted by Newman, the *Letter to the Duke of Norfolk* contains statements on conscience which are 'acknowledged by all Catholics'. Newman merely set down the Catholic theology of conscience in a clear and concise way.

When confronted with a teaching which one may feel to be in error, or would go against one's conscience to obey, one should not undertake a decision to follow one's conscience against the teaching of the pope lightly. One should give serious thought, prayer and make use of all available means of arriving at a right judgement on the matter in question. The initial point of inquiry must rule out the possibility that it is merely a case of misunderstanding the voice of the pope which is leading to a conscientious objection. Once this has been ascertained not to be the case, one's moral disposition must be examined. This is similar to Newman's conscience in its true sense of the word, and not a 'counterfeit' which becomes a licence to 'be his own master in all things, and to profess what he pleases, asking no one's leave, and accounting priest or preacher, speaker or writer, unutterably impertinent, who dares to say a word against his going to perdition, if he likes it, in his own way.'[3]

What one must bear in mind when speaking of the supremacy and inviolability of the individual conscience and its rights when found to be in conflict with magisterial authority, is that it be a true and educated conscience. Conscience, when true, is the voice of God within us. Once established not to be 'counterfeit', it must be followed even if in conflict with authority. The Episcopalian philosopher Alan Donagan, recalling Newman's toast, notes: 'were we obliged to bring morality into toasts, we should not refuse to drink to conscience; but we should beg to drink to a truthful conscience first.'[4]

A new questioning

It is perhaps the contemporary emancipated female Catholic who, having moved away from her traditional role of mainly wife and mother, questions the authoritative role of the church and the role of the individual conscience, the loudest and longest. Women now not only shape their own home lives, but also wider society through their active involvement in the workplace. In the past three or four decades, they have been consciously transformed by returning female emigrants, the media, and an increasing control of their fertility. Several facts reveal this new independent Irish Roman Catholic woman – the widespread use of artificial contraceptives, the increase of births outside marriage, and the increase in legal separations and divorces initiated by the female spouse. This evidences the deepening gulf between women's consciences, their actions and the church's moral teachings. For many reflective, practicing female Roman Catholics, current church teaching on marital sexuality in particular causes pain and alienation. Because Irish women were traditionally more religious than the Irish male, society at large feels the repercussions of this conscientious estrangement. Many women are no longer instrumental in the handing on of an unconvincing faith in the home, and are practising their own faith less within the formal church environment. Education in the faith for the young Catholic is now relegated to the Catholic school and to a lesser degree, the parish. If the majority of Roman Catholics now depend upon their judgement of conscience for moral action, and not the teaching of the church, and perhaps choose contrary to what is taught, it is imperative that they fully form and inform their conscience to the best of their ability. It is the duty of the whole Christian community to educate our younger members, be it through an established Catholic education system, parish activities, or by our own behaviour.

The forming of conscience
The Catholic educator has an important responsibility towards the formation and education of the young conscience, especially in a secular society where there is apathy towards religious and ethical formation. Education of the human person who is on a life-long process of creative learning and growing in Christ, is initiated by the lived morality of parents and others, and contin-

ued formally in the classroom. It is important, therefore, that we teach young adults to correctly and confidently use their Christian conscience in moral decision-making. The Catholic educator is not only the religious educator, but is also the teacher of those other humanities subjects such as English, philosophy, history, media and biology. These areas also raise questions about the human condition and the reality of life, including moral issues which call for a judgement of conscience on the part of the student now or in later life. The Catholic educator is also predominantly a lay Catholic because religious are no longer present in many schools. The contemporary religious education teacher has also trained in a different atmosphere than in previous decades. Increasingly, theological studies are offered in secular providers of third level education, and not only in the traditional ecclesiastical institutions. Lecture halls are filling with lay, predominantly female, theology students, being taught by lay theology lecturers. Theology itself is becoming secular. No longer is it dominated by ecclesiastics doing a doctrinal theology from within the church. Instead, theology has begun to converse with other branches of knowledge, and looks at issues from outside the church, seeing faith resources in secular culture. Our religious lives have moved from a separate section of our lives, that special world of the divine, to join with our everyday historical world. God and the church should be a part of this everyday, ordinary world. Our Christian beliefs should permeate our fundamental disposition towards others. It is important to allow valid cultural influences to encourage a practical theology which will enable our teachers to present a convincing and motivating faith context for the education, training, practice and experience of conscientious moral decision-making. The true conscience is enabled and matured by informing and educating it, for we are not born with a conscience, but with a capacity for conscience. We inform our primitive conscience through reason and experience, those human sources of knowledge, and also through the divine sources of knowledge: holy scripture and tradition. It is also important to be attentive and respectful to the authentic teaching authority of the church, and not regard it as merely one opinion among others, for the church declares natural moral principles determined by God, understood in the light of faith.

In order to make a sincere and correct conscientious decision, we must be convinced that our conscience has all the available information. If we are in doubt in any way as to what our conscience is commanding or forbidding us to do, we must not act according to it. A wilfully erroneous conscience is objectively wrong and culpable. This type of conscience makes an error in judgement through lack of effort or will to overcome any naïveté or ignorance. We must endeavour to overcome any ignorance we may have by being aware that we are limited by our human finitude and sinfulness. Though our reason and past experience may inform our conscience about a given situation, we may not have all the facts, nor fully grasp all the implications of an action. We may also be under the overt or covert influence of personal or social sin. We must be open to any guidance available to us, be it through prayerful dialogue with God, church teaching or other branches of knowledge. Similarly, there should be recognition that there may be limits to the use of the bible or Christian tradition due to cultural conditioning or historical context. Scripture has incorporated many cultural meanings over time – even some that are erroneous. We could use the historical example of women's inferior position in the Christian church and society to illustrate. Christian feminists often highlight how the bible incorporates the social and familial patriarchy of the times in which its books were written. For example, the household codes found in the New Testament record contemporary cultural attitudes towards women. These codes, found primarily in Colossians 3:18-4:1 and Ephesians 5:22–6:9, document the inferiority and subordination of women to men. Man is, they claim, the head of the household, and a woman is to obey her husband. For centuries, these teachings perpetuated women's subservience in the Christian church. However, due to a deepening understanding of sexual equality and knowledge of the importance of the female experience, we now recognise that such teaching is wrong and must be corrected. Moreover, scripture does not deal with the many new issues that we are now facing in different historical and cultural circumstances throughout the world. It does not, for example, address issues of nuclear power, reproductive technologies or genetic engineering. As Christians, we must inform and educate our consciences to the best of our ability in order to live morally upright lives modelled on Christ.

We must be careful not to over-emphasise any one or more of our sources of knowledge to the detriment of the others. All must act as controls. It is important to recognise that a true and informed mature conscience may sometimes find itself in disagreement with an official church or secular principle of general application. These conflicts should be regarded as an important source of moral insight into the new dilemmas which give rise to such conflicts. The church must acknowledge the responsible and faithful attitudes taken by those who engage in these conscientious moral decisions which result in dissent from official teaching. There must be a reaffirmation of the inviolability of the individual true conscience and its importance in the ongoing search for truth.

CHAPTER TWELVE

The Celtic church and lessons for the future

John Scally

The past is a different country. The Ireland of St Patrick was radically different from the society we are so familiar with today. At first glance the Celtic church which he initiated all those years ago may appear to have little to say to us today. However, the noted American theologian David Tracy has told us that one of our key theological tasks is to achieve a 'mutually critical correlation' between the Christian tradition and contemporary experience. In that context it may be instructive to consider what the Celtic church, itself a very imprecise term, has to teach us in the Ireland of 2005. Such a task must be approached with a 'handle with care' warning or in more theological terms 'a hermeneutic of suspicion'. There is a danger of an excessively misty-eyed approach to the 'golden age of Irish Christianity'. This era was not without its dark spots. To take just one example, the early monasteries were very often under the control of local chieftains and there were quite a few examples of monasteries going to war with each other. One of the problems with the Irish church at the time was that it was so identified with local lords that the original Christian impetus was lost. Sometimes the monasteries became little more than pawns in the local wars going on between the local chieftains. Nonetheless, notwithstanding the enormous social, economic, cultural and political differences between the early years of the third millennium and the period of the fifth and ninth centuries of the first millennium, could it be that, in some respects, our future is in our past? Could it be that the Celtic church had some significant emphases which we could profitably retrieve to the enrichment of our society today?

Hospitality

Unlike subsequent monastic settlements, the Celtic monastic communities were open to all. They were places of hospitality, where the marginalised were welcomed. Hospitality was often very much in the tradition of the story of the widow's mite. Although they had very little to offer, they gave generously. They seemed to share the view of St Francis of Assisi that it is in giving that we receive. They were centres of sanctuary, where safety was guaranteed.

St Brendan was one person particularly associated with hospitality. He was born in 483 or 484 CE. He was fostered by the famous St Ita (who had a special gift with children) from the age of two until five, in Killkeedy near Newcastle West in County Limerick. She was known as 'the foster-mother of the saints of Ireland'. It is said that Brendan asked her what were the three things that God especially loved. She replied 'God loves a true faith in him with a pure heart; a simple life with a religious spirit; and open-handedness inspired by charity.'

The tradition of the 'Ireland of the welcomes' can be traced back to pre-Christian times. Under the Brehon laws, to refuse hospitality was not simply impolite, it was considered an offence. The arrival of Christianity gave a new impetus to this tradition. In the judgement gospel (Mt 25) hospitality is seen as an integral part of the Christian life; 'I was a stranger and you welcomed me.' Hospitality was actually institutionalised in the Irish monasteries with each having its own *Teach Aíochta* (house of hospitality). The monks supplied food, drink and overnight accommodation to all passers-by without seeking any financial donation.

In the Celtic tradition, the guest was always Christ, and hospitality was offered to the Christ in the other. One story which illustrates this is told about St Crónán. He had an unexpected visit from a neighbouring abbot and a large entourage of his monks. While they were eating at table, a young novice caused a bit of a stir by saying aloud, 'It seems there will be no vespers said here this evening.' After a short, awkward silence St Crónán responded, 'Brother, in the guest is received Christ; therefore at the coming of Christ we ought to feast and rejoice. But if you had not said that, the angels of God themselves would have prayed on our behalf here this night.'

St Brigid's monastery in Kildare was known as the City of the Poor, on foot of its reputation for hospitality, compassion and generosity. These were genuinely inclusive communities. Brigid is the perfect example of Irish hospitality: she could (miraculously) milk her cows three times in one day to provide a meal for visitors. Brigid celebrated the God who dances. She was no killjoy, going so far as to describe heaven as a great lake of beer. According to the conventional belief at the time, St Brigid had no interest in material things because her focus was solely on God.

St Brigid was able to see Christ in other people. A famous story told about her illustrates this. Brigid had embarked on a long journey and she stopped to rest by the wayside. A wealthy woman heard that she was in the locality and brought her a beautiful basket of apples. As soon as the apples appeared, a group of people came by and begged for food. Immediately Brigid gave them the apples. Her benefactor was aghast and barked disdainfully, 'I brought those apples for you, not for them.' Quick as a flash Brigid replied, 'What's mine is theirs.'

Familiar strangers?
The 'Ireland of the hundred thousand welcomes' is still marketed by the tourist industry, but in some respects this Ireland has been buried in a pauper's grave. Indeed our travelling community might well have grounds to ask was it ever anything but a figment of our imagination. Given the apartheid, Irish style, to which they have been subjected, they must find the phrase 'fellow citizens' nothing more than a bad joke.

However, surely the biggest blight on Irish society in the last decade must be our treatment of asylum seekers. The xenophobia that has emerged in certain sections of our population in recent years is very disturbing. Listening to the many phone-ins that dominate our airwaves, it is evident that the attitude of many people towards ethnic minorities continues to worsen. Even more shameful is the fact that a handful of politicians, including two sitting TDs from the main government party, have cynically whipped up the frenzied paranoia some people have about the asylum seekers issue as a cheap way to solicit votes.

The late Brendan Behan once went into a bookshop and saw a copy of the *Catholic Standard* and remarked: 'Ah, here is the news of the next world.' This is a revealing observation, highlighting as it does the way in which many Christians think of the church's purpose, i.e. to prepare our souls here in this world for the next world. The Celtic church knew otherwise, in the way it publicly aligned itself with the poor and the outcasts. The Celtic church was a radical presence which empowered all people to have a meaningful life.

Service was very prominent from its earliest days, and in later centuries it was arguably a contributory factor in the failure of the Reformation to take off in Ireland, because the monks were catering for the material needs of the marginalised as much as for their spiritual needs.

Our Christian vision must remain very critical of all those projects which do not allow all people to participate. In the bible the question of where and how we can serve the Lord has an unambiguous answer. We find him in the hungry, the thirsty, the stranger and the naked, we see him wherever people are in need and cry out for help. The Christian God revealed to humankind in a definitive way in the bruised and broken body of the suffering Jesus, continues to reveal himself wherever human suffering is to be found. The Celtic Christians were people who recognised God in the course of their daily care to others. The heart of their discipleship was the ongoing discovery of God's presence in the midst of the human struggle.

More than words
Celtic Christianity was literally down to earth. It had no sense of a two-kingdom spirituality or of a rigid dichotomy between the secular and the sacred. The Gaelic language ensured that the

most mundane of social intercourse became occasions of prayer. In the Celtic tradition people are blessed every time they say goodbye in the phrase *Go mbeannaí Dia dhuit* (God bless you). The standard greeting to friend and stranger was *Dia is Muire dhíbh.* (God and Mary be with you.) What is particularly instructive is that many of these greetings are in the plural, as the presence of Christ in the other is also acknowledged.

God was understood as appreciative of, and protective of, every single human life. The Celtic description of a disabled person as God's own person *(duine le Dia)* is a good illustration of that point. In the Celtic tradition old life, injured life, disabled life, every life is God's own life, God's special gift and task. Sadly, as campaigners like Kathy Sinnott constantly remind us, to be disabled in the Ireland of 2005 is not to be cherished. From the beginning she had to fight tooth and nail for every resource for her son, Jamie. Her experience was that Jamie did not get resources as a matter of right. She spent years fighting every arm of the state to try and give Jamie the best possible start in life.

Successive governments have failed to provide the necessary infrastructure to support our more vulnerable citizens. In 2002 the government attempted to railroad a Disability Bill through the Oireachtas and in the process demonstrated the utter contempt which exists in the halls of power for those requiring support. The proposed Bill did not include any rights for those with a disability. This same contempt has been shown time and again to carers, pensioners and those on waiting lists for a range of necessary hospital and specialist procedures.

One of the buzz phrases today in social and political life is the 'democratic deficit' – the frustration 'ordinary people' experience because they are denied any real power in the society in which they live, having little or no say in the decision-making processes. For disabled people the possibility of making decisions for themselves is often little more than a pipe dream. Decisions about their welfare are often taken by people who have no direct experience of what it is like to be disabled.

The problem is resources, or more precisely, lack of re-

sources. Many medical and technical advances have presented
new and exciting treatment options – the use of art and music
therapy to help people cope with mental illness are innovative
examples. However, there is a major shortage of funding, which
leaves many disabled people seriously disadvantaged. It is too
easy though to talk about action for disabled people in terms of
aspirations, but lip service fails to yield any practical benefits.
What are needed are specific targets and specific action programmes. To take a practical example, the Inspector of Mental
Hospitals, Dr Dermot Walsh, in his annual report observed
about one particular hospital in Leinster: 'The whole situation in
the admissions unit was intolerable and could not be condoned.'
Almost a third of the patients in the hospital had 'an intellectual
disability and required specialist care in an intellectual disability
facility' and 'were inappropriately placed'. Parents were 'not
satisfied with aspects of privacy and dignity of care in the admissions unit'. There are many thorny legal and ethical problems in the area of mental illness, notably in the involuntary in-
carceration of patients and the validity of consent to particular
forms of treatment. The problems are exacerbated by the fact
that much of the legislation in this area is very old, e.g. the Trial
of Lunatics Act 1883. In this area, like many others, we must
strive for legislation which maximises the fulfilment of rights
and minimises their violations.

Incredibly, in the Ireland of the Celtic Tiger there are many
people with disabilities whose lives could be transformed with
basic treatment – but there is insufficient money available. To
take a practical example, the ability to talk easily and communicate is one of the most important social skills a person needs, but
in the Ireland of 2005 there are many people who are literally living lives of quiet desperation because of a stammer. Our economy
is awash with money, but the amount of resources needed to
help people in this situation, through the provision of an ade-
quate speech therapy service, is relatively minor. It is not that it
is going to be a growing expenditure in the years ahead. Since it
is not a disease or a physical disability, some people think that it

is relatively unimportant, but it can have a huge effect on people's self-development.

To take another specific example: young blind and visually impaired female pupils are being forced to travel to Northern Ireland for their education due to the lack of facilities in the Republic. One fifteen-year-old girl from the west of Ireland who spends her weekdays as a student in Belfast is fostered on weekends because it is impossible for her to travel home every weekend. It is incomprehensible that in these days of conspicuous national wealth such a situation is allowed to develop and continue.

When some are less equal than others

For all our talk of equal rights, a significant minority of people living in Ireland have not achieved legal, economic or cultural parity. The economic, political and cultural disadvantages suffered by these 'outcasts' are serious violations of justice. It cannot be disputed that the Ireland created by the Celtic Tiger is a much more prosperous one. Yet this creates dilemmas of its own. Contemporary society displays a proliferation of many needs – individual, social, environmental and medical, each demanding a fair share of society's scarce resources. Unfortunately, there are not enough resources available to meet all those needs. There is no easy ethical blueprint to which society can refer to establish that all of its obligations have been justly discharged. In the context of difficult decisions about the distribution of resources, awkward questions are raised. How is the tension between the rights of individuals and the overall good of society to be resolved? What are the relevant inequalities that justify giving more of the scarce resources to some and less to others? Clearly we require a balance between the rights of the individual and the good of the other and the common good; but how in the Ireland of 2005 are we to attain that correct balance? To date we are failing a significant element of our population.

A number of questions present themselves about the place of disabled people in 2005. In Irish society, are all people equal, or are some, like the disabled, seen as less equal than others? How many disabled people are institutionalised? How many have a home of their own? How many have access to the special education that they may require? How many have a job? The Celts knew how to cherish the disabled. By our actions, and often inactions, we do not.

Amongst women

In the sixth century St Brigid's foundation was unique in that it was a double monastery for women and men. Each group followed the same rule and used a common church, with the government of the whole community held jointly by the abbess and the bishop-abbot. This was one of those rare periods in Irish church history when women were given a meaningful role and could claim to have equality.

Pope John Paul II's *Mulieris dignitatem* (The dignity of women) in 1988 noted that one of the recommendations of the 1987 Synod of Bishops was for a 'further study of the anthropological and theological bases that are needed in order to solve the problems connected with the meaning and dignity of being a woman or a man'. Unfortunately that challenge has not been adequately taken up. A new approach is needed to take account of the need to build new relationships of mutuality and reciprocity between women and men in the church. Today, people's faith is threatened by many factors, including poverty and family break-up. Many women, however, feel that their faith life is endangered by a patriarchal church.

Despite a massive amount of equality legislation, many women echo the type of sentiments expressed by Mary Robinson in her inauguration speech as Irish president in 1990: 'As a woman I want women who have felt themselves outside of history to be written back into history, in the words of Eavan Boland, finding a voice where they found a vision.'

The Celtic web of life

The Celtic understanding of the divine was never merely of a transcendent presence but also an immanent reality in people's everyday lives. While they did retain the traditional Christian doctrine of a transcendent God, i.e. the God who watches us from a distance, the Celtic Christians laid particular emphasis on the immanence of God, i.e. the closeness of God to us and his involvement with nature and with the world, a vital presence in the world, animating all of creaturely life. They saw creation as offering a window into God. Columbanus stated, 'If you want to know the Creator, understand created things.' This heavily experiential understanding of God was beautifully summed up by An tAthair Donnchadh Ó Floinn as a 'breathing in and breathing out of God'. Seamus Heaney has written about the legendary story of St Kevin praying with outstretched hands for so long that a blackbird came to make a nest and lay an egg in one of them. According to Heaney, at that moment Kevin was 'linked into the network of eternal life'. The literature of the early Irish Christians is full of celebration of the fact that God and nature are closely intertwined. *The Voyage of Brendan*, for example, is the story of Brendan's quest to find the Promised Land of the Saints.

In Celtic times it was believed that all wells had their source in one great well deep inside the centre of the earth. These were sacred places, guarded by protective feminine spirits. In this tradition a rainbow was understood as a love letter from God. The theologian John Macquarrie claimed that the Celts were 'intoxicated with the love of God'. Celtic Christians clung to the tradition of the holiness of nature, which it had subsumed from the pre-Christian Irish tradition. St Patrick's contemporary, Pelagius, contended that nature was incorruptible and Duns Scotus Eriugena would later claim that the living body of Christ is in the world and not in the church, as God is in all things.

Of course, this stress on the immanence of God's ongoing creative project in everyday life did lead to distortions in the same way as theologies which placed heavy emphasis on the transcendence of God neglected his immanence. Nonetheless, it placed the emphasis on the presence of a divinity in the world, eternally co-creating. The paths of nature and spirit kissed, creating a web of life between people, creation and God. Heaven and earth forged an intimate alliance. Humankind and creation were not just God's playthings, but partners in God's creative project. The theology which underpins Celtic Christianity is emphatically incarnational. Of course the bible itself is radically incarnational, when the Word was made flesh and Jesus of Nazareth came as the human face of God. Celtic Christianity was also Trinitarian and this fascinating combination of emphases had a major influence on the religious imagination.

The value of the person was seen as inviolable only when the human person is understood as a creature of God. The personal meaning of life can only lie in religious communion with God. The mystery of God is a reality which pervades all of our creaturely life. This worldview was later taken up by the mystic, Meister Eckhart, who believed that 'outside of God there is nothing but nothing'.

Caring for the earth

Many of the early Irish monks were filled with missionary zeal. Among them were people like St Killian who went to Germany. It would be fascinating to investigate the extent to which these early Irish monks may have sown some of the seeds of the modern green movement. For example, one of the people who would have inherited the spiritual tradition of these early monks was Hildegard of Bingen, who was born in Böckelheim, Germany in 1098 to a noble family, the tenth of ten children. From an early age, mystical experiences formed an integral part of her life, and it may have been on account of these visions that her family sent her, at the tender age of eight, to the care of a Benedictine monastery. In due course she became a Benedictine sister herself and in 1141 she received the divine command to record her visions.

What is most startling to the contemporary eye is the relevance of her message, despite its antiquity, to the concerns of today. Particularly fascinating is her insight into what in today's parlance is termed 'creation spirituality' – best summed up in

her use of the concept of *viriditas* or greenness, which is representative of the creative power present in nature and in humankind, and having its ultimate source of expression in God.
Humankind, despite its special place in creation, has a special
responsibility to nature, and abuse of our position would upset
this dynamic of interdependence. Accordingly, she showed that
humankind is entrusted with a caretaker role. She claimed:
'Although creatures have been made in order to serve our
needs, we too are answerable to them.' These sentiments represent to a considerable extent the spiritual inheritance of Celtic
Christianity and they still have an important message for today.

Love actually

Apart from their relevance to the wider society, the Celtic
Christians have much to offer us to reflect on in our spiritual and
personal lives. Their spirituality was deeply scriptural and it is
interesting to read the prayers they composed, and observe in
them their great love of the scriptures. They were also very
imaginative, as is evident in their rich artistic legacy, including
the *Book of Kells*, the Derrynaflan chalice, remnants of wall paint-
ings in certain churches and the high crosses. Could the Irish
church today benefit from an infusion of such creativity and
imagination?

'That's only a contemplative order' is a phrase one sometimes hears today when people are talking about religious life.
Apart from what it betrays about our understanding, or lack of
understanding, about religious life, it surely says something
about our attitude to prayer. It is as if prayer is on the periphery
of the Christian life, instead of at its very centre. Perhaps this attitude is a symptom of the times we live in, an age which values
achievement rather than reflection. In the hustle and bustle of
our everyday lives, it is often difficult to find the inner stillness
to make space for God to speak to us. From the number of people listening to walkmans or talking on mobile phones while
travelling on bus or train, it seems that we abhor silence. Yet the
Celtic church embraced it as was reflected in the large number of

hermits. They appreciated the value of solitude because they saw it as a fertile state of mind and spirit in which it is possible to concentrate on something for a fairly long time and also to establish a relationship with the object of our concentration.

The poetry of the early Celtic Christians shows their willingness to meditate on the qualities that made them deeply human and also relate to the superhuman. The problem of their sexual nature is a recurring theme in the poetry of the early Irish monks, and the challenge they faced was to transform their sexual energy into religious energy. Of course this is not to imply that the religious and sexual are mutually exclusive, but they treated their sexual longings in such a way that those feelings were converted into a longing for God. This of course is not unique. One of the greatest poets in the English language, John Donne, was a very accomplished metaphysical poet and went on to become a great religious poet.

Brendan Kennelly translated many of the poems written by the first Irish monks. One was a short poem called *The Bell*, which furnishes us with a revealing insight into the preoccupations of our Celtic forebears:

I'd sooner keep my tryst with that sweet little bell,
the night of a bad winter mist,
than risk a ravenous female.

It is a very strong poem, with very definite anti-woman feelings. Yet it equally shows that the Celts gave full attention to their human nature. In this way they inspire us to reflect on both human relationships and whatever relationship we have with what is beyond the human.

Dying and behold we live

The Celtic understanding of the cycle of life and death is crucial to the inner growth of the soul. In the Celtic tradition, each new day is seen as a new beginning, a gift from God. Today this insight needs to be retrieved. Ours is an age which is obsessed with youth. The growth of the cosmetic surgery 'industry' reveals that so many people seem petrified of aging, let alone dying. We need a new culture of dealing with the reality of death. The Celtic tradition has many insights to offer to this debate. Columbanus wrote in one of his sermons, 'I am always moving from the day of birth until the day of death.' St Brendan echoed a similar sentiment. Death is not the end of the story, but another phase in the soul's journey, an entrance into the wider life, endlessly stretching out. As Christians we ought to be in the forefront of the development of this new understanding of death, as we profess to believe that the eternal life into which we pray to be resurrected has long begun.

CHAPTER THIRTEEN

Embryonic stem cell research: a new frontier

David Smith MSC

The scientific and popular media have heightened expectations about new wonder therapies that will develop from stem cell research. This research is often presented as one of the new frontiers in science. The crossing of new frontiers by science and technology is one of the characteristics of humanity; and freedom of research is an important, hard-won value in Western culture. Nevertheless, science and technology are not autonomous and value-free. They take place in a cultural, social and environmental context and should be servants of humanity, not its leaders. Stem cell research and therapy may alleviate human suffering, yet important questions need to be asked about whether or not the hoped-for benefits are proportionate to the research itself.

Stem cell research

Human stem cell research and therapy raises many ethical problems. Some of the most acute issues have to do with the different sources of stem cells. In principle, stem cells can be obtained from adults, from umbilical cord blood, from foetal tissue and from embryonic tissue. Clearly there are widely differing views as to the ethics of sourcing stem cells in these four different ways. Currently, the general consensus is that human embryos are the best source of stem cells for therapeutic purposes, but this may change as the science develops. There is also the question of whether or not embryos or foetuses may be deliberately produced, either by in vitro fertilization (IVF) or somatic cell nuclear transfer (cloning), in order to be sources of stem cells.

Obtaining stem cells from adults, umbilical cord blood and

foetal tissue have ethical issues specific to them, such as consent, patenting issues and the transfer of information. However, it is the issue of stem cells from human embryos that is most vigorously debated. This is due to the fact that embryonic stem cells have to be generated from embryos that are destroyed in the process. Stem cell research again raises the question of whether there are any ethical limits concerning the destruction of human embryos for research or therapeutic purposes, as well as the more fundamental question of the moral status of human embryos. If human embryos have any moral status, a proportionate justification is needed to destroy them.[1]

The question of the moral status of the embryo was not resolved during the abortion debate or during the debates about various forms of assisted reproductive technologies. It is, therefore, unlikely to be resolved during the current debates about stem cell research.[2]

Another significant issue is one of women's rights. Women are the most proximate sources of embryonic and foetal material and may encounter unique pressures and indeed risks if they are to be sources of stem cells.

Free and informed consent is an additional ethical concern for both the donors and recipients. Particular attention needs to be paid to appropriate ethical standards in the conduct of the research on human subjects. There are issues of the anonymity of the donors, the security and safety of cell banks and the confidentiality and privacy of the information they hold, as well as the tissue they contain. There are issues of commerce, remuneration and patenting for those taking part, and of the transport and security of human tissue and genetic material and information across frontiers, both within the European Union and worldwide. Finally there are interesting paradoxes concerning the ethics of benefiting from research many regard as morally suspect or evil, should the research bear fruit.[3]

Scientific basis
Stem-cells are primitive cells that are responsible for creating

various tissues and organs in the body. At an early stage in their development, stem cells are unspecialised. This means that stem cells are uncommitted cells, capable of dividing to make more stem cells or, under appropriate conditions, to produce the kinds of specialised cells that make up the tissues and organs of the body. The newly fertilised egg is the ultimate stem cell. It is totipotent – capable of generating all the different types of cells found in the body, and also the foetal part of the placenta and supporting tissues. Stem cells from the sources above differ in a number of ways; one way is the plasticity of the cell, which refers to the range of cell types that the cell can turn into. All embryonic stem cells have high plasticity as they develop into all the different organs and tissues of the early foetus, such as arms, legs, blood vessels, kidneys etc. It was thought that older cells and tissues, such as adult stem cells, had very limited plasticity, but recent research has shown that adult cells also have plasticity and can even turn into cells of another type (e.g. adult nerve cells may be able to turn into blood cells), a process called transdifferentiation.

After birth, stem cells only reactivate when new cells are needed e.g. after injury. Under certain conditions, they may become cells that can develop into almost all types of cells or tissue. They can also undergo self-renewal – that is they can divide to form further unspecialised stem cells. As already mentioned there are different sources of stem cells:

Sources of stem cells	Name
Early human embryos	Embryonic stem (ES) cells
Aborted or miscarried human foetuses	Foetal stem cells
Umbilical cord blood	Placental stem cells
Adult humans	Adult stem cells – bone marrow (or haematopoietic); skin; blood.

Already stem cells are used in research trials to treat adult neurological diseases such as Parkinson's disease and Huntington's disease (so-called foetal stem cell therapy, where donated cells from an aborted or miscarried foetus are inserted into the brain and grow to replace the deficient chemicals produced in these diseases). Some cancers can also be treated by bone marrow stem cells, commonly called bone marrow transplants, which are infused or transplanted into patients who have leukaemia or lymphomas. The stem cells replace the abnormal leukaemia cells with normal blood cells – these are called haematopoietic stem cells and have been in hospital use for over three decades.

Adult cells grow much more slowly than embryonic cells. So researchers prefer to use embryonic cells for faster results. Recent research has shown that what had originally been promising results on replacement of heart cells by adult stem cell work cannot be replicated,[4] so the hope that adult stem cell research may provide answers and treatment is further away than previously thought, and is unlikely to result in treatment for some decades.

Governmental responses
Despite all the research carried out on stem cells to date, little is known as to how and why embryonic cells grow much faster than adult cells. Thus the need for more research. This, in turn, has led to Governmental interventions. In the United Kingdom, the Fertilisation and Embryology Act (1990), based on the recommendations of the Warnock Commission, allowed scientists to research on embryos up to the age of fourteen days. This research was usually limited to issues concerning aided reproduction. In 2001 the United Kingdom authorities passed the Human Reproductive Cloning Act to prohibit cloning for human reproduction. However, the authority of the Human Fertilisation and Embryo Authority was extended to allow it to licence research on embryos specifically created for research, either through normal in vitro fertilisation therapy or through somatic cell nuclear transfer. In 2004 the first therapeutic cloning licence was granted to the Centre of Life Sciences at Newcastle University. By separ-

ating the issues of reproductive and therapeutic cloning, the United Kingdom authorities banned reproductive cloning while allowing therapeutic cloning. Therapeutic cloning means that a cloned embryo would be created so that its stems cells could be developed to produce specific tissue which could then be used in the treatment of an individual patient who is genetically identical to the cloned embryo. In 2003, the United Nations General Assembly failed to pass a treaty on human cloning despite agreement that cloning for reproductive purposes should not be permitted. This failure was due to linking both reproductive and therapeutic cloning, and the differences of opinion regarding the moral status of the embryo.[5] Within the European Union divisions on the ethics of embryonic stem cell research is apparent: Sweden, Finland, Greece and the Netherlands permit it, while other EU states (Italy and Austria) remain strongly opposed to it.

In the USA investigators are currently prevented from using federal funds to do new research to develop stem cells from early embryos. In 2001, President Bush stated that he could not condone the destruction of embryos to generate stem cell lines and placed a four-year moratorium on the generation of new stem cell lines. A further bill is currently before the House of Representatives to outlaw, in the private sector, the cloning of embryos.

Theological basis
A theological foundation to resource their deliberations is needed by Christians when attempting to morally evaluate human embryonic stem cell research. In the Christian faith, the universe exists as a result of God's creative activity and of his 'over-abundant grace' (St John Damascene); it always depends on his beneficent will. Human beings are part of creation, but they have a special position in it: man and woman are created 'in the image of God' in order to 'have dominion over' creation (Gen 1:28). There is a tension between Genesis 1 and Genesis 2. In the light of Gen 2:15 'dominion' is not to be interpreted as domination but rather as a vocation 'to work and to care for' the earth,

i.e. to reflect God's creative and caring relationship to the world. It may be interpreted as a vocation to responsible stewardship in the world.

Traditionally, when exploring an ethical dilemma, Christians have referred to the wisdom of the scriptures and the Christian tradition to illuminate their deliberations. But, when considering some of the ethical issues which human stem cell research raises, it is not possible to draw directly on the scriptures or tradition. This presents new challenges and opportunities to theology for understanding within constantly changing social circumstances. Yet it is also important to take into account the plurality of opinion, not only in society, but also within the churches, when considering these issues.

In the context of recent developments in biomedicine and biotechnology, 'playing God' is a frequently used expression. From the perspective of Christian faith, its meaning is ambiguous: it may be argued that humans, created in the image of God, are called to be responsible stewards in the world. Mostly, however, the term is used to point to the aspect of going beyond the bounds of human limitations, by assuming a role that is not ours to have. According to this notion, humans have neither the understanding nor the foresight to take sufficient care and responsibility to perform genetic modifications. There is certainly a need to follow developments critically, but extreme attitudes, that nothing is allowed or everything is allowed, are not justified. What should be asked is whether recent developments in biomedicine and biotechnology infringe or support basic ethical and social values, and whether they may be seen as a responsible use of our skills and our attitude towards creation.

Another way of viewing these developments theologically is from the perspective of liberation. Will stem cell research provide instruments for the liberation of human persons from suffering? Does this proposed research enable human persons to fulfil their potential with dignity? Are human persons facilitated to participate justly with their fellow human beings in community? Finally, are the natural bases of human existence such as identity, freedom and common humanity, safeguarded? If stem cell research does not ultimately lead to the liberation of the person then the opposite would apply. Such domination and alienation of the person is ethically unjustifiable.

The ethics of human embryo stem cell research

Does human embryo research to develop stem cell lines transgress a new ethical barrier? Present research for infertility still treats the embryo as a reproductive entity, for the long-term benefit of other embryos. This type of research into diagnostic methods and reproduction is permitted, to varying degrees, by a number of Christian churches. However, it is research into the development of embryo stem cell lines for therapeutic purposes which is provoking heated discussions. Is there a moral distinction between these two forms of research? To use an embryo as a source of body cells is a very different notion as it treats the embryo purely functionally, as a resource and no longer as a whole entity. If the embryo came to be seen as a routine source for replacement cells, it would be difficult to see how its 'special status', referred to in governmental and church documents, could be retained. However, many thousands of 'spare embryos' no longer wanted in IVF treatment are destined to be destroyed. Many feel that to use these for research into embryonic stem cells would be better than destroying them. Research into potential therapies is not qualitatively different from research into diagnostic methods or reproduction. Neither benefits the embryo upon which research is conducted, but both may be of benefit to people in the future. Each form of research involves using the embryo as a means to an end but, since many accept the morality of doing so in relation to currently authorised embryo research, there seems to be no good reason to disallow research on the embryo where the aim of the research is to develop therapies for others. Resorting to the argument of the lesser of two evils, some Christians consider that it is justifiable to use *existing* 'spare' embryos in potential treatments for serious diseases, if they would otherwise be destroyed.

The fact that embryo stem cells potentially have valuable

applications in a wide range of diseases raises the question of whether increased demand might lead to the creation of embryos specifically for research. The purpose of this research would be the obtaining of embryonic stem cells and creating immortalised cell lines. Such a development might be seen as a step towards commodification of the embryo and one that denies the embryo the respect it should be accorded.

Is there an ethical distinction to be made between the use of a donated spare embryo for the derivation of embryonic stem cells and the use of an embryo specifically created for this purpose? A donated embryo has been created with a view to implantation in the uterus. Once it is not implanted, it no longer has a future and, in the normal course of events, it will be allowed to perish or be donated for research. It can be argued that the removal and cultivation of cells from such an embryo does not indicate lack of respect for the embryo. A donated embryo will have been created for use in a reproductive technology programme where the goal is a successful pregnancy. If it is unsuitable or intended to be discarded, its use for the derivation of embryonic stem cells will not alter its final disposition. Alternatively, embryos could be created through in vitro fertilisation (IVF) from donated gametes (ova and sperm) with the sole purpose of producing cell lines. Such an instrumental use, where the embryo is essentially a means to an end, does not accord with the respect owed to a potential human life.

An additional concern refers to women's rights. If stem cells are to be produced from embryos that are not 'spare' after IVF, the ova for this production must come from women. In the initial research phase the number of ova needed will be relatively small, but for stem cell therapy, the number may become very large. This raises general problems concerning how society can ensure that the ova are obtained without coercion or exploitation of the ova donors, sellers or providers. Another question to be addressed is about how a new practice of non-reproduction related ova procurement would influence the status of women in society.[6]

What about cloned embryos for research? Somatic cell nuclear transfer often referred to as cloning, as in the case of *Dolly* the sheep, can be achieved in the following way. An ordinary specialised adult cell from the patient could be used to produce a totipotent stem cell by removing the nucleus (with the DNA-containing chromosomes), and inserting it into a human egg from which the nucleus has been removed. If allowed to grow, this foetus would be genetically identical to the adult from whom the adult cell was taken. There has been almost universal condemnation by the churches and social representatives of the cloning of human beings for reproduction. It is also important to note that the development of animal cloning to date has shown a widespread pattern of problems in pregnancy, foetal abnormalities and early deaths of newborn animals. This makes it quite clear that, for the foreseeable future, it would be foolhardy to attempt to clone human beings, quite apart from the very strong ethical objections. The use of somatic cell nuclear transfer to create embryos of the right genetic type, now permitted in some jurisdictions, to produce replacement cells presents further ethical dilemmas.

As already observed, there are ethical objections to the creation of embryos specifically for the development of stem cell lines. Cloning adds an additional objection. It seems illogical to allow the creation of a cloned human embryo knowing full well one would have to destroy it on ethical grounds, because it was unethical to allow it to go to term to produce a cloned baby. Then there is the gradualism or slippery slope argument. Opponents of this technique have claimed that allowing this would put society on a slippery slope towards reproductive cloning. The slope that is imagined is of a technical nature. If all the technical problems in the first steps of somatic cell nuclear replacement techniques are solved successfully, then it becomes easier and more tempting to try to use nuclear replacement techniques for reproductive cloning.[7]

Consent

In all jurisdictions couples undergoing fertility treatment must specify or consent to the uses that can be made of embryos created from their gametes, including whether or not the embryos can be used in any research project. This implies that couples must be given a suitable opportunity to receive proper counselling about the implications of taking the proposed steps and they must be provided with relevant information so as to make an informed decision.

The use of embryonic tissue in research projects to establish embryo stem cell lines raises issues relating to consent that are different from those raised by other forms of research. Although the establishment of a cell line will involve the destruction of the embryo, the DNA (deoxyribonucleic acid) in the cell of the embryo has the potential to exist indefinitely in laboratory conditions. The cells could be ultimately used in a wide range of therapeutic applications and, with DNA testing, such a cell line could theoretically be traced back to the individual embryo donors. The theoretical potential to trace the source of a cell line is not unique to embryonic stem cells, but applies to any cell line established from donated tissue. Consequently, where specific research regarding the establishment of an embryonic stem cell line is contemplated, embryo donors should be asked explicitly whether or not they consent to such research and subsequent use of the cell line.

Patenting

As research has progressed the issue of patenting has become an ethical issue. Recently a United States patent was granted on 'cells which come from the early human embryo and are pluripotent', which in effect means that in the USA all human embryonic stem cells are now subject to a monopoly of one company. This would appear to contravene fundamental ethical principles. Patenting of stem cells should not be permitted for the following reasons. The cells of the human body are the common heritage of all people. All such cells are discoveries and not inventions as is normal in patenting products. They have merely been isolated from an embryo or adult tissue, or allowed to differentiate from the resulting stem cells. They are in no sense a human invention. The potential for treatments is extremely wide, constituting an entire new area of medicine. It would be contrary to the concept of *ordre publique* to give anyone a broad monopoly over what may prove to be an entirely new way of treating a wide range of otherwise incurable human diseases. A number of studies have shown the deterrent effect on research which was caused by granting very broad patents at the early stages in the development of some otherwise promising new areas of biotechnology. Stem cells represent an area where the maximum encouragement should be given. To permit patenting could retard research and, more importantly, limit access to the results and benefits of this research.

Benefiting from an immoral act
If a person professed that the destruction of embryos to develop stem cell lines was unethical, could he/she ethically receive a therapy which was developed from these stem cell lines? The problem of benefiting from evil or co-operating with evil received some attention during the 1980s and 90s in connection with the issue of using research results from immoral Nazi medical experiments.[8]

An important point in this discussion is the connection between the uses of goods produced through evil and the encouragement of wrongdoing in the future. There seem to be three ways that individuals who make use of goods produced by wrongdoing might encourage the commission of evil deeds. First, there is direct encouragement though agency. A person is asked to commit a wrongful deed on behalf of another. Consequently the commissioning agent benefits from the person's wrongdoing. A second kind of encouragement involves direct encouragement through the acceptance of benefit. No agency relationship exists. One person independently undertakes an evil deed, and for whatever reason, a second person

experiences some benefit as a result. The third kind of encouragement is called indirect encouragement through legitimis-
ation of a practice, or practice encouragement. The best example
of practice encouragement arises in connection with the use of
the research results produced by Nazi doctors. Why should researchers today not use that information to improve health or
save human lives? Using this data establishes and legitimises an
undesirable public rule. 'Researchers may use scientific information that has been created by wicked research on human subjects so long as 1) the information can benefit humanity and 2)
there is no chance that those who created the information will be
encouraged to repeat their deeds.'[9]

When these principles are applied to stem cell research and
its potential benefits, it is important to remember that, at present
and in the foreseeable future, embryo destruction is entirely independent of stem cell research and therapy. Surplus or spare
embryos are routinely created in the practice of infertility treatment. These are either stored for a limited period of time or destroyed. Using these surplus or spare embryos for embryo stem
cell research does not cause the death of these embryos; the decision to discard them does that. Research causes only the manner
of their destruction.[10]

It can, therefore, be argued that none of our three types of encouragement referred to need occur when someone uses a stem
line derived from these spare embryos.

It may be possible for even the staunchest opponents of
human embryo research, in good conscience, to use stem cell
lines for research or therapeutic purposes. The key assumption
is that the destruction of the embryos needed for this purpose
has occurred (or will continue to occur) unless infertility procedures change. Yet, for those opposed to embryo research, this
excludes the use of embryos deliberately created for this purpose, whether by sexual fertilisation or cloning.[11]

Conclusion

Referring to the principles of the 'lesser of two evils' and 're-sponsible stewardship' it can be argued that it would be ethical to permit embryo stem cell research on spare or surplus em-bryos because they are already destined for destruction. The hoped for results of the research and potential benefit for suffer-ing people are proportionate to the method of destroying spare embryos. The deliberate creation of embryos for research, either through the IVF technologies or cloning, appears to merely view the embryo as a source of replacement cells and that is more dif-ficult to ethically justify.

Perhaps a more nuanced approach would be to permit a limited number of embryo experiments so as to obtain the data necessary to avoid embryo destruction in the future.

CHAPTER FOURTEEN

Must the poor always be with us?
A new model for a global economy

C. Denis Kelly

The critical characteristic of today's world is an obsession with power for its own sake, to the detriment of the common good. Nevertheless, it is fair to say that every revolution or *ism* is a striving for better times, and sets out with the best intentions. American democracy was a reaction to feudal and religious persecution, communism to labour exploitation, totalitarianism to economic collapse, and modern tribalism to political and religious discrimination. As each ideology grows strong, its potential for exploitation is recognised by those in power. What drives this consuming obsession with power? Could it be more than natural greed? Is it manageable? By reverting to first principles and building anew, the answers to these questions emerge.

The free market economy

In a free market economy dominance and consequently, dependence, is the predominant ethos. An important contributor to this economic dominance has been the rapid acceleration of scientific research which preceded and then fuelled the Industrial Revolution. It changed civic society, transforming pre-industrial social values by creating an urban social class wholly dependent on others for employment and survival. The civic horizons of these dependent people narrowed and, in time, virtually disappeared. Understandably, they were replaced by daily considerations of personal and family survival. Power is still popularly understood as economic power.

Scientific research, an admirable expression of human endeavour, is largely in commercial hands. The products of its research, particularly in the fields of medicine and food are, on occasions, marketed without the examination of their down-stream effects on the complex and delicate balances in nature. Genetically modified food, for example, is a cause for wide-spread concern. Artificial fertilisers are another product group the emerging side effects of which are now being countered by legislation. There is little doubt that more fundamental research needs to take precedence over the development of endless new products for the market, even if the resultant research and de-velopment costs are higher.

The pressure exerted by commercial interests on educational facilities, particularly evident at third level, is relentlessly forc-ing a move away from educating for life, and towards greater technical specialisation; it empowers the students, without educ-ating them to use their new knowledge responsibly.

Damaging business practices
The most evident damaging business practices are at the con-sumer level and involve the misuse of effective, valid communic-ation techniques to distort the market in favour of 'want' over need. Psychological and emotional vulnerability is exploited, and a widespread discontent is generated among those who cannot afford to buy. Social deprivation may also result when scarce funds are diverted away from needs in order to satisfy created 'must have' wants. This may be called a free market economy, but how free is it? The international spend on weapons, alcohol and tobacco, cosmetics and entertainment each far ex-ceeds that of Third World aid. This is hardly a deployment of resources for the health and happiness of all humanity.

The financial institutions, too, are complicit in promoting in-flationary consumer debt. Rarely are savings plans promoted with the same intensity or enthusiasm as are loans. Money in the form of debt is inflationary and is now also an entrenched ele-ment of world economics which demands ever increasing con-sumption.

Conflict is also an economic 'opportunity'. In the time of the slave trade, West African tribes would not sell their friends and relations to the slavers. Prisoners of war were a different matter, however, so the slavers gave the tribes guns and ammunition to solve the 'problem' of the supply of slaves for the Americas. The arms manufacturers still thrive today on the misery of African tribal conflict.

The world's media play an important part in moulding public opinion to their own imposed, or supplied, agendas. At times, truth has nothing much to do with what they print, broadcast or otherwise disseminate. With news media increasingly being taken over by entertainment conglomerates, 'news as entertainment' is a disturbing new trend.

Corporate growth is such that national boundaries can no longer contain it. National control of corporate behaviour is ineffective on the global scene and new forms of bigger and better exploitation and domination abound, aided and abetted by national governments. In this material environment, everything is methodically designed to oil the wheels of profit generation. Life is measured by material success only; it is competitive, adversarial and ruled by the written law, which can be at variance with natural justice.

The international protests at WTO, IMF and G8 meetings are evidence of a growing discontent with this ruthless material philosophy, as is the growth of organisations like Greenpeace and Earth-watch. If unbridled materialism is not moderated, the widespread opposition to it will intensify. The way we live seems to preclude an effective solution to this fearful discontent. There is a growing sense of unease and frustration in the lack of a clear understanding of what must be done. There is undoubtedly a subconscious – or even a conscious – fear at the dominant level of what might be required to correct it, and how disruptive and costly it could be. It is not unreasonable to conclude that the world has lost its way and it knows it. In this condition, minor adjustments to the system may relieve some of the pain some of the time, but will not address the underlying problem of domination and exploitation. The answer to this problem of consumerism/materialism must have the recognition of the overall good of the person in nature as its basic premise.

The person in nature

Today's rampant individualism challenges our social nature. It devalues the family, the fundamental unit of society, and crudely measures personal success in material terms, while ignoring the human cost often borne by others. In the wider context too, the human species is not the team player in nature it should be. There is a blind assumption that the world is ours to exploit. There are delicate balances at work in the universe, and the life systems on which we depend for our existence are part of them. We interfere with them at our peril.

Can we overcome our frenetic materialism and consider our role as social animals in a much bigger and inter-dependant system? It will be difficult in a world that is so busy, so noisy and so philosophically confused. Few would argue with the proposition that the way we live ought to be determined by the overall good of the person in nature. With this criterion, let us look at how a range of familiar situations could change.

The family's paramount place would be restored and its needs would take precedence over material gain. Education in the family is where the foundations of citizenship and sociability are laid. Where the family needs help, or where it has fallen apart, the requisite love, care and support would be otherwise provided, for as long as necessary, to ensure opportunity in life for all. Formal education would then reinforce social and civic values, not only as a subject, but also through the ethos of educational institutions. Education for life would dominate at all levels throughout the educational process, and its values would carry strongly into subsequent citizenship and parenthood. The position of the teacher as an essential person in society would be resolutely preserved, and the profession's structures would lead the way in the continuous self-improvement of its members.

The ways people are governed would change to serve the needs of each person. The development of his or her social and intellectual potential would dictate policy. This can only happen when public representatives are freed from conflicts of interest. This proposed new order would create opportunities for a review of civil and criminal law. The concept of the 'common good' would keep the needs of the person in nature as the prime consideration. The emphasis would be on judging people's actions as they affect the common good and on helping them to appreciate their civic responsibilities. When the common good must be protected by taking a person out of circulation, that person would get remedial help which, if successful, would permit his or her return to the community

Intelligent and transparent co-operation between organisations of influence and those controlling resources, which heretofore competed for dominance, would prevail. Government services, religions, utilities, business and commerce could all make important contributions. Business would still flourish, but its focus would be to serve the needs of the market and then the interests of its shareholders. Human nature being what it is, some recognition would have to be given to entrepreneurship and creativity, so that success in which others can share is rewarded. Incomes would still vary but the lower levels should improve while excessive incomes should moderate. For example, tax bands might be set at multiples of the minimum wage. The cynics and detractors will be quick to reject all of this. But the same world with a global human focus is not as impossible as it might seem.

The current Western economic system drives people to behave in an unacceptable way. There are trustworthy and responsible people everywhere and their better instincts can triumph if our economic systems are conducive to this. Business, professional people, and politicians are products of our present value systems. Not all of them will want to lead the change to something that could be perceived to be against their interests. The real drive for change must ultimately come from ordinary people. In Western democracies, ruling political parties, who are beholden to those who fund them, talk down to the people whose input is minimised to voting every few years. This is a serious reversal of roles. Active political involvement by the people is the essence of true democracy. There have been a number of experiments to achieve this, of which the outstanding example is the Participative Budget Process (PBP) in Porto Alegre, capital of Rio Grande do Sol, Brazil.

Porto Alegre – a practical example

Commencing in 1989, the manner in which the discretionary element of the Porto Alegre's budget of $500 million should be spent has been decided by the people. The success of this initiative has been such that the participatory approach has been adopted by many other cities throughout Brazil. The Programme has been referred to by the UN as a model for development.

The stated objectives of the PBP are:

1. To promote democracy and the capacity of the citizen to determine the future.
2. To promote law in the city through citizen participation.
3. To listen to the citizens, either individually or collectively and on a permanent basis.
4. To make the public sector a tool in the hands of the majority of the population.
5. To control and distribute the tax revenue paid by all the citizens.

The legal basis for the PBP is defined in the Federal Constitution (1988) and in the State Constitution (1989), which define Brazilian democracy as a representative and participative democracy, pursuant to article 1 that states: All power emanates from the people, who use it through elected representatives or directly.

This process has been put in place with the singular purpose of achieving truly democratic participation by each district in managing its own affairs. It is totally inclusive in that the poorest and least educated and the more fortunate work together in the interests of their districts and of their city. In Porto Alegre, the PBP runs from March to December. (The initial budget planning takes place in January/February.) The city is divided into sixteen districts for the purpose of distribution of resources. In each district there are dozens of meetings – some very large – and working parties tackle specific tasks. In a typical year, the process involves over a thousand agencies and over forty thousand people. The PBP directly decides how 15% of the total budget is spent and broadly shapes the allocation of another 25%. The remaining 60% is largely devoted to the salaries of city employees.

Methodology

When the draft budget is drawn up at local government level, it is presented to various community institutions and organisations representing health, education, transport, arts, etc, who debate the details and make suggestions before it goes back for definitive approval. In this way the budget is not simply imposed after having been debated by the politicians, but is exposed to thorough examination and feedback from the sectors that are directly affected by it. While this slows the decision-making process, it results in more relevant and effective decisions about how to apply limited resources.

To quote from one of the city's many descriptive and promotional leaflets:

The PB is becoming a practical tool of democracy. The open discussion of the problems faced by each street and neighbourhood, the standardisation of criteria for the use of the budget, the ranking of priorities establish a two-way relationship; the city administration accounts for expenditures, proposes projects and carries them out; the community raises problems, discusses them and decides where public money is to be invested, following the whole process.

Outcomes

The specific outcomes of the PBP are complex, since they involve so many aspects of the life of the city. Porto Alegre still has many of the problems associated with extremes of poverty and wealth existing side-by-side. However its citizens acknowledge that their city has been transformed. Its finances are sound. It has one of the most comprehensive and best equipped public transport systems in the world. The investment in transport has been integrated with the widening of the main avenues and the building of hundreds of kilometres of pavements in the poorer and remoter neighbourhoods.

The World Social Forum, January 2002 Conference (delegates from over 200 cities in 29 countries attended) reported that 'Porto Alegre has a literacy rate of 97%. 100% coverage of refuse collection, including recycling. 92% of residents are connected to mains sewage, 99% to mains water. There are forty Family Health programmes, whose staff visit the poorest homes to offer protective services and advice on domestic hygiene. More than 3000 needy families receive financial assistance and psycho-social services.' It is also said that crime has greatly reduced, as the citizens have a sense of ownership and take a more propri-etorial attitude to anti-social behaviour.

The Participatory Budget Process is an initiative of the Brazilian Workers' Party. As a political initiative, it is generous and grounded in common sense. Education has an important part to play in helping people to become more discerning citi-zens and electors. The PBP is an educational process of the great-est value in achieving this critical capability. (For those who would like to know more about empowered participatory gov-ernance, I recommend *Deepening Democracy: institutional innova-tions in empowered participatory governance,* by Archon Fung and Erik Olin Wright, New York, Verso, 2003, and also *The Porto Alegre experience,* by Marion Gret and Yves Sinotomer, London, Zed Books, 2005).

The role of money
The common element in all economic activity is money. It meas-ures economic success, it oils the wheels of growth and it facili-tates the exchange of goods and services in the market. However, the present monetary system has some serious draw-backs. For all practical purposes, money always comes with debt; it carries interest charges, which inflate at each level of dis-tribution and are passed on to the ultimate consumer. This is an inflationary process. Furthermore, a monetary system based on

debt, and in which there are competing currencies, creates its own market. There is currency trading on a massive scale, which adds no value to the economy, and is only of interest to the economically dominant. Consequently, the values of currencies fluctuate, hurting the weaker economies most. In this environment, business cannot fulfil its primary function of supplying the needs of the market. Instead it is forced into financial profitability and a crushing drive for continuous growth which is unsustainable in a finite world. It would appear, therefore, that a reform of the monetary system would be a logical step towards freeing human endeavour to serve the common good.

A proposal for monetary reform
It is argued that the fundamental roadblock to progress towards the provision of the needs and the realisation of the potential of all people is the monetary system in which money is interest-bearing. The conflict between money as a traded product and money as a facilitator of exchange of goods and services results in a 'casino culture', which favours individualism and the concentration of wealth in pursuit of power and domination, be it at the personal, corporate or national level. This ignores the social nature of humanity, only services its needs when it is sufficiently profitable to do so, and prevents the realisation of its collective potential and well being. Monetary reform is, therefore, a prerequisite to progress.

To overcome this distortion of purpose, the interest-bearing nature of money must change to a currency that is debt-free and is exclusively a facilitator in the exchange of goods and services. This could be achieved by the creation of a Monetary Authority with responsibility for the distribution and management of an interest-free currency.

Operation of the Monetary Authority
The Authority would regulate the money supply to balance the goods and services available for purchase and the capital requirements of human needs. The distribution of money could be

done through the culturally appropriate provision of basic purchasing power for everyone in serious need, thus eliminating endemic poverty. This, in turn, would generate local enterprise and employment. It would also facilitate the provision of education, health, and research independent of the private corporate sector where investment is driven by profit potential and patent protection rather than priority need. Furthermore, it could provide pension schemes for all, which could be augmented privately from savings to the upper income limit, thus removing the fear of old age and the large families that are seen by many as an insurance against destitution. World population growth would moderate in consequence.

Capital requirements for industry and commerce would be provided, without cost, for properly researched projects, thus avoiding the inflationary effect of interest in the cost of goods and services. The Monetary Authority's investment in such projects could be protected by equity holdings in the form of preference shares, and of the control of dividend policy while any debts remain outstanding.

Local Government would be financed locally, but where this might be impossible, the necessary funds should be made available to ensure needs are met and to hasten local development to self-sufficiency. To facilitate the control of money supply and to obviate anti-social activities, systems should be in place to deter the accumulation of money outside the Monetary Authority, in any circumstance.

At the personal level, incomes should not be open-ended. There is compelling evidence that happiness is not income-related after sufficiency is achieved. Furthermore, the greater the disposable wealth, the greater the human greed. It is proposed that the spread between minimum and maximum incomes be controlled, possibly determined as a multiple of the regional minimum wage. This need not inhibit the accumulation of personal wealth so long as it is in productive form, or held in holding accounts in the Monetary Authority for productive investment within a reasonable period, after which or on death it would return to the Authority. Inheritance should require some distribution of productive ownership to the stakeholders in its creation. The needs of the ego could be served by public recognition in culturally appropriate forms.

At corporate and government levels, funds over and above working requirements should be lodged to holding accounts, or otherwise taxed heavily. This would guard against investment in socially subversive and potentially divisive activities, such as the means to exploit and dominate others. To avoid the accumulation of illegal funds, the Monetary Authority could, from time to time and without notice, issue notes of a new currency. Notes in circulation would not be exchanged, but pre-determined amounts equivalent to what would be reasonably required for current needs would be credited to personal and corporate accounts in the Authority.

Ideally the Monetary Authority should evolve into a Global Monetary Authority, with a single currency worldwide, but it will have to start on a regional basis. To get started, the pioneering region(s) will require a significant place in international trade, which will force the rest of the world to acknowledge the new currency and trade in it. The resulting economic and social success generated by debt-free finance will have a powerful influence on people still struggling under the unjust and discriminatory debt-bearing monetary system. In this initial period, it is important to keep Paulo Freire's wise words in mind and struggle to bring everyone forward without rancour to a fairer and more rewarding society in which all humanity can participate in accordance with their differing cultures and personal capabilities.

The management of the Monetary Authority

Who should manage the Monetary Authority? It is proposed that this could be done by a group of suitably qualified people representing all major cultures. It is important that what is decided and implemented should be acceptable and adaptable in differing cultures and to their evolving needs, so that growth and self-sufficiency are achieved without disruption to familiar ways of life.

Methods of election and rotation of these qualified and culturally representative people need careful determination. It is imperative that all major cultures are fairly represented at all times. A national approach is unlikely to work, as nationalism and 'national interest' is driven by self-interest. Salaries should be within the generally accepted norms and expenses realistic, so as to attract people with the right values, who have concern for 'the overall good of the person in nature' as the basic criterion. Economic development planning and project assessment capabilities would have to be provided in all regions, in addition to banking and accountancy skills, if personal income, wealth records, inheritance distribution and investment activities are to be transparent. This mammoth task is only now possible with the new, rapidly developing IT skills available.

This proposal is designed to help industry and commerce to focus on providing the needs of humanity and to give everyone access to his/her basic needs as a matter of natural right. This natural right has somehow been lost, and lost sight of, in the growth of urbanisation, private and corporate ownership and personal wealth creation.

Basic needs

At the personal level, the basic needs of food, clothing and shelter would be restored to everyone. This would be carried into old age as basic pensions, which could be augmented from personal savings. The family, however it is defined in differing cultures, would be respected as the smallest unit of society and facilitated accordingly. Health and education would be provided to help in the realisation of everyone's well being and social potential. The money supply would be controlled, not by arbitrarily limiting the supply of money to the market, but rather by continually removing surplus money from the market. This would ensure that the needs of the human race rather than those of 'the economy' are met as the priority. The realisation of human potential could proceed without interruption. Salaries would be set within a scale to reward ambition and entrepreneurship (e.g. minimum wage x 20). Income above this maximum would be very heavily taxed if not lodged in personal holding accounts in the Monetary Authority for socially desirable investment. Capital would be made available for both house purchase and local small enterprise development.

At the corporate level, interest-free investment capital would be available, as would the benefits of skills training and re-search, so as to facilitate growth and efficiency in supplying the needs of the market. The distorting demands of investors for continuing and escalating profit generation would no longer be a dominant issue, and such activities as asset stripping and job losses in favour of cheap labour in developing regions would not be options. Corporate incomes above working needs would be managed in a similar fashion to excess income at the personal level, and be available for investment in productive projects, or in the social and community areas of health, education, research or academic studies.

At the community or regional levels, the Monetary Authority would fund major infrastructure, while local government would be assisted where necessary to reach a practical level of local self-sufficiency so that local development is not retarded.

The differing degrees of development in the world's economies would be recognised and protected, if they are all to be able to achieve a measure of self-sufficiency. Import duties on problem products between regions could be a useful mechanism of control. Furthermore, corporations with global ambitions would be required to vest ownership/control locally in any facility and in the product and brand they establish in a region other than their own. This would protect people from exploit-ation in regions with particular short to medium term economic attractions, like low wage rates and poor labour and environ-mental law.

Patent rights, which reward research investment, can also be used in anti-social ways. Curable diseases are a case in point where cost prevents cure. Research would be better carried out by a research agency financed by the Monetary Authority and with regional/global responsibility, totally removed from any commercial considerations. Private research could be undertaken on projects and at a cost agreed with the research agency. Patent law would then be dispensable.

It is argued that the well being of the human race, as a responsible team player in nature, would be significantly enhanced in the wake of this monetary reform.

A Global Monetary Authority

Consider the ultimate scenario in which a Global Monetary Authority (GMA) issues a single debt-free currency into circulation. It could:

1 Keep the money supply and the world's goods, services and investment needs in balance.
2 Release new money, debt-free, to the money supply on the basis of regional population and need, and thus create basic purchasing power, local development and job opportunities for those in need.
3 Provide funds for appropriate capital projects, e.g. schools, hospitals, road/rail infrastructure.
4 Provide basic pensions schemes for all, which could be augmented from personal savings.
5 Control financial activities in the private and public sectors by removing from circulation excess earnings and private income above appropriate levels. These monies would then be available for investment. This would encourage an emphasis on the production of needs, as spending power would be more evenly spread. It would also encourage investment in education, job creation, social services, and academic studies including research and development, and facilitate the GMA in the control of the money supply.
6 Encourage the intelligent use of the world's non-renewable resources.
7 Provide debt-free funds to the private sector for productive investment, suitably secured.

8   Provide debt-free loans for house buyers with personal savings of a defined minimum, as appropriate.
9   Provide bridging finance to local authorities, as special needs require; otherwise, local authorities should fund themselves locally.

It will be asked: 'Who will control the Monetary Authority?' The question arises from a mindset that thinks in terms of national interest, whereas the Authority's focus will be regional or global. Its staff must be professional and represent all major cultures involved to ensure that the criteria agreed are capable of being culturally conditioned.

Conclusion
This proposal is hardly operable as long as there is strong economic nationalism, in which war and 'free' trade are viewed as legitimate options. This reform proposal addresses this problem by ensuring that everyone has basic purchasing power, and the means through which they can realise their individual and community potentials. To research and develop the (Global) Monetary Authority concept, a group of multi-cultural economists and other specialists is needed, representing large populations, at least some of whom have persuasive levels of international trade. If the financial system could be simplified and freed from intrinsic value, the reforms required to achieve 'opportunity for all' would be much more attainable.

Notes

CHAPTER ONE

1. *Does morality change?* Dublin, Columba Press, 2003, 121-126.
2. Ibid, 21.
3. 'The new approach to seminary training,' *The Furrow*, vol 16, n 5, May 1965, 267-276.
4. 'The theological formation of the seminarian,' *Irish Ecclesiastical Record*, vol CV, n 5, May 1966, 302-313.
5. 'Religious life in a new millennium,' *Religious Life Review*, vol 41, n 216, September-October 2002, 284-295.
6. A letter by Mrs Mary McAleese (now Úachtarán na hÉireann) to *The Irish Times* in January 1995 on the *Intercom* controversy is worth reproducing: 'What is truly depressing about this episode, though, is the contrast between the energy and determination which went into sorting out a perceived problem with the editorial tone of *Intercom*, and the sheer breath-taking ineptitude of church handling of matters relating to child abuse by clergy. It is truly ironic that Father Kevin Hegarty raised the issue openly in *Intercom* long before the Father Brendan Smyth affair, and in so doing incurred the wrath of those so anxious now to reassure us of their clean hands and *bona fides* in this squalid business. Well, so be it. The script is all too familiar. Another resounding triumph for fear-filled mediocrity. Whatever happened to the Good News?'
7. 'Religious & sex abuse cases,' *Religious Life Review*, vol 31, n 157, November-December 1992, 317-320.
8. 'How can I stay in this corrupt church?' *Religious Life Review*, vol 41, n 217, November-December 2002, 358-364.
9. 'Abused nuns: questions to answer,' *Religious Life Review*, vol 40, n 208, May-June, 2001, 146-156.
10. 'The Institutional and the charismatic,' *Religious Life Review*, vol 33, n 165, March-April 1994, 66-75.
11. 'The Laity: our sleeping giant,' *Doctrine & Life*, vol 37, n 1, January 1987, 2-8.
12. 'Confession outdated?' *Doctrine & Life*, vol 24, n 8, August 1974, 407-417.
13. '*Humanae Vitae* in perspective,' *Doctrine & Life*, vol 43, n 7, September 1993, 426-430.

14. '*Humanae Vitae* 30 years on,' *Doctrine & Life*, vol 49, n 1, January 1999, 51-54.
15. 'Divorce: a possibility for Catholics?' *Doctrine & Life*, vol 22, n 12, December, 1972, 625-635.
16. 'Catholic divorce?' *Doctrine & Life*, vol 53, n 4, April 2003, 229-238.
17. 'The Church and the homosexual: a response,' *Doctrine & Life*, vol 30, n 8, October 1980, 409-420.
18. 'Homosexuals are God's holy people,' *Religious Life Review*, vol 42, n 220, May-June, 2003, 141-146.
19. Siobhán Foster-Ryan and Luke Monahan, eds, *Echoes of suicide*, Dublin, Veritas, 2001, 209-215.
20. Ibid, 212.
21. Ibid, 215.
22. *Irish Theological Quarterly*, vol XXXII, n 1, January 1965, 64-66 (book review).

CHAPTER TWO

1. Irish Bishops' Conference, 'Notification on recent developments in moral theology and their implications for the church and society,' July 2004, at www.catholiccommunications.ie/ PastLet/ index.html.
2. Charles E. Curran, *The Moral theology of Pope John Paul II*, Washington, Georgetown University Press, 2005.
3. For a detailed explanation of the Lutheran paradoxical approach, see H. Richard Niebuhr, *Christ and culture*, New York, Harper & Row, 1951, 170-85.
4. Maurice Schepers, 'An Integral spirituality of the paschal mystery' *Worship* 75, March 2001, 98-106.
5. Richard P. McBrien, *Catholicism*, rev. ed., San Francisco, Harper, 1994, 9-12.
6. Andrew M. Greeley, *The Catholic myth: the believers and beliefs of American Catholics*, New York, Charles Scribner's, 1990, 36-64.
7. Sixtus Cartechini, *De valore notarum theologicarum et de criteriis ad eas dignoscendas*, Rome, Gregorian University Press, 1951.
8. For a recent discussion of these issues by two cardinals, see Kilian McDonnell, 'The Ratzinger/Kasper Debate: The Universal church and local churches,' *Theological Studies* 63, 2002, 227-50.
9. www.e-paranoids.com/i/in/in_necessariis_unitas_in dubiis_ libertas _in_omnibus_ca.html,
10. Gérard Philips, 'History of the constitution,' in Herbert Vorgrimler, ed., *Commentary on the documents of Vatican II*, 5 vols., New York, Herder and Herder, 1967, I, 109.
11. Pope John Paul II, *Tertio millenio adveniente*, nn 133-36, in *Origins* 24, 1994, 401 ff.; *Incarnationis mysterium*, n 11, in *Origins* 28, 1998, 450-51; 'Jubilee characteristic: the purification of memory,' *Origins* 29, 2000, 649-50.

12. John T. Ford, 'Pope John Paul II asks for forgiveness,' *Ecumenical Trends* 27, December 1998, 173-75; Francis A. Sullivan, 'The Papal apology,' *America* 182, no 12, April 8, 2000, 17-22; Aline H. Kaliban, 'The Catholic church's public confession, theological and ethical implications,' *The Annual of the Society of Christian Ethics* 21, 2001, 175-89.

13. Jaroslav Pelikan, *The Vindication of tradition*, New Haven, Conn., Yale University Press, 1984, 66. For my development of this point, see Charles E. Curran, *The Living tradition of Catholic moral theology*, Notre Dame, Ind., University of Notre Dame Press, 1992.

14. Theodore Mackin, *The Marital sacrament*, New York, Paulist, 1989, 274-324.

15. For Pope John Paul II's discussion of faith and reason, see his encyclical *Fides et ratio*, in J. Michael Miller, ed., *The Encyclicals of Pope John Paul II*, Huntington, Ind., Our Sunday Visitor, 2001, 833-913.

16. James H. Provost, 'Pastor bonus: reflections on the reorganization of the Roman curia,' *Jurist* 48, 1988, 499-535.

17. John Connery, *Abortion: the development of the Roman Catholic perspective*, Chicago, Loyola University Press, 1977, 223-303.

18. Thomas Bouquillon, 'Moral theology at the end of the nineteenth century,' *Catholic University Bulletin* 5, 1899, 267.

19. Charles E. Curran, ed., *Change in official Catholic moral teachings: readings in moral theology No 13*, New York, Paulist Press, 2003.

CHAPTER THREE

1. Wilfrid Harrington, OP, 'Scribalism in the church,' *Doctrine & Life*, vol 23, n 6, June 1973, 298-304.

2. Medieval scholastic theology had long been in decline. In the nineteenth century Leo XIII sought to revive it. His encyclical *Aeterni Patris* recommended that scholasticism be the only philosophy and theology used in Catholic seminaries. This neo-scholasticism was, in essence, a Christian Aristotelianism. It tended to be rigidly conceptual. Basic data such as revelation, faith and tradition were narrowed down to concepts which were regarded as static, treated as things and almost separated from Christian experience. It was ahistorical in its approach, oblivious to the cultural conditioning of theological statements. It operated, in practice, independently of scripture, at best using scripture uncritically as proof-texts. Under Pius X neo-scholasticism was confirmed in theory as the theology of the church. Merely to suggest an alternative theology or to question neo-scholasticism became subject to ecclesiastical sanctions. Indeed, there was a veritable witch-hunt of 'deviant' theologians. The only 'true' theology was that of the Roman curia. This unhappy situation remained up to Vatican II.

3. Anthony J. Saldarini, *Pharisees, Scribes and Sadducees in Palestinian*

society: a sociological approach, Wilmington DE: Michael Glazier, 1988. John P. Meier, *A Marginal Jew, Vol. 3, companions and competitors*, London, Doubleday, 2001, 549-560.

4. Meier, op. cit., 80; see 549-560.
5. Daniel Harrington, *The Gospel of Matthew*, Collegeville MN, The Liturgical Press (A Michael Glazier book), 1991, 327.
6. Mark Schoof, *Breakthrough: beginnings of the new Catholic theology*, Dublin, Gill & Macmillan, 1970.
7. Ibid., 149-150.
8. Ibid., 151.
9. Franz König, 'My vision for the church of the future.' *The Tablet*, London, 27 March 1999, 424-426.
10. *Lumen Gentium*, chap 1, n 8.
11. Christi potestas et imperium in homines exercetur per veritatem, per iustitiam, maxime per caritatem. III. Sent.d.13, q.2. (Christ's power and rule over people is exercised through truth and justice, and most of all through charity).
12. Edward Schillebeeckx, OP, *Church, the human story of God*, London, SCM Press, 1990, 222.

CHAPTER FOUR

1. Andrew Greeley, *The Catholic revolution*, California, University of California Press, 2004.
2. Peter Steinfels, *A People adrift: the crisis of the Roman Catholic church in America*, New York, Simon & Schuster, 2003.

CHAPTER FIVE

1. Donal Dorr: 'Sexual abuse and spiritual abuse,' *The Furrow*, vol 51, n 10, October 2000, 523-531.
2. David Lodge, *How far can you go?* London, Secker & Warburg, 1980.
3. French psychiatrist Pierre de Salignac, a dedicated Catholic, wrote a book entitled *The Catholic neurosis*, SCM, London, 1982, describing the psychologically harmful effects of church teaching on sexuality. While official teaching shows little signs of change, today's theo logians present a very different, more human and sensible approach. An excellent example is Donal Dorr's book, *Time for a change: A fresh look at spirituality, sexuality, globalisation and the church*, Dublin, Columba Press, 2004.
4. Cf. Seán Fagan, *Does Morality Change?* Dublin, Columba Press, 2004, especially chapters 8 and 9.
5. Ibid., chapters 6 and 7.
6. Joseph Ratzinger in Herbert Vorgrimler, ed., *Commentary on the documents of Vatican II*, vol V, 134.
7. Paul Lakeland, *The Liberation of the laity: in search of an accountable church*, New York, London, Continuum, 2003, 193.

8. Jack Dominian, *Living love – restoring hope in the church*, London, Darton, Longman, Todd, 2004.

9. Wilfrid Harrington OP, 'Scribalism in the church,' *Doctrine & Life*, vol 23, n 6, June 1973, 298.

10. Eamon Duffy, *Faith of our fathers*, London, New York, Continuum, 2004, 166-167.

11. Cf. Bernard Häring, *My Witness for the church*, New York, Paulist Press, 1992. An excellent brief discussion of this problem is chapter 18 of Eamon Duffy's *Faith of our fathers* (What about the Inquisition?). Some seven examples are discussed in *From inquisition to freedom*, by Paul Collins, New York, London, Continuum, 2001.

CHAPTER SEVEN

1. Madeleine Bunting, 'Family fortunes,' *The Guardian*, 25 September 2004 (supplement, part three: ourselves in the year 2020).

2. Austin Flannery, OP, ed., *Vatican Council II: the basic sixteen documents, constitutions, decrees, declarations*, Dublin, Dominican Publications, 1996, 221-222.

3. I use this term reluctantly as I would like to argue that there is as much difference between persons of the same sex as between persons of the opposite sex.

4. *Catechism of the Catholic Church*, Dublin, Veritas, 1994, 2357.

5. Joseph A Komonchak, Mary Collins, Dermot A. Lane, eds., *The New dictionary of theology*, Dublin, Gill and Macmillan, 1987, 624-628.

6. A situation described on 'Dinner with Portillo' BBC 4, September 2004.

7. For a further exploration of some of these ideas see: Anne Thurston, 'Expanding the language of love', *The Furrow, vol 54, n 12*, December, 2003.

CHAPTER EIGHT

1. Most of the affirmations in this chapter deserve further comment. The resulting reading would be burdensome, so I am following the advice of Harold Acton in his *The Bourbons of Naples*, London, Prion Books, 1998, xvii. 'The cult of the footnote, involving, at its apogee, a page crammed with encyclopaedic details in small type to a solitary line of text, is no doubt a proof of diligence, but it may also be a tedious form of exhibitionism.' Some bibliographical indications may still be helpful for those who wish to question my opinions or follow up a particular point. I mention a few, more or less in the sequence of the points made. For official church teaching, a useful starting point is *Homosexuality and the magisterium: documents from the Vatican and the U.S. bishops 1975–1985*, John Gallagher, ed., Mt Ranier, MD, New Ways Ministry, 1986. Later documents, such as the Letter to Bishops on the pastoral care of homosexual persons

(dated 1 October 1986) published by the Sacred Congregation for the Doctrine of the Faith can be consulted in the *Acta Apostolicae Sedis*; the periodical *Origins* often provides an English translation of the main documents. For a sense of the variety in the homosexual community in Ireland there are many interesting contributions in *Coming out: Irish gay experiences,* Glen O'Brien, ed., Dublin, Currach Press, 2004. I have found useful material on the typology of homosexuals in the writings of the Italian moral theologians E. Chiavacci, G. Piana and G. Rossi, none of them available yet in English, unfortunately. The effort to see a closer link between liturgy and moral questions has been nourished by reading some works of Don E. Saliers, particularly his *Worship as theology: foretaste of glory divine,* Nashville, Abingdon Press, 1995. Understanding the church takes me back, when I am sensible, to the works of Yves Congar. For this chapter I re-read one of his slighter books, *The Revelation of God,* London, Darton, Longman, Todd, 1968. I find confirmation of these insights in the *Pastoral Constitution on the Church in the Modern World,* 1965, which is the key text of the Second Vatican Council for understanding complex moral problems in the light of the gospel and of human experience. I hope, too, that the implications of how moral principles might be applied has been nourished by the *Praxis confessarii* written by Saint Alphonsus Liguori in 1755; it retains the freshness of the practical wisdom of this Doctor of the Church even after 250 years and in a very different type of church. One learns not just from books: I have ministered, as a priest, to groups of homosexual Catholics in five countries and I acknowledge what they have taught me about the metaphorical complexity of a question that seemed to me, in my early priestly innocence, among the easiest to answer.

CHAPTER NINE

1. N. Ammerman, 'North American Protestant fundamentalism, in M. E. Marty and R. Scott Appleby, eds., *Fundamentalists observed,* Chicago, Chicago University Press, 1991, 2.
2. J. Kent, 'Newman and Lilley,' in *John Henry Newman and modernism,* A. H. Jenkins, ed., Sigmaringendorf, Verlag, Glock & Lutz, 1990, 164.
3. J. Hitchcock, 'Catholic activist conservatism in the United States,' in Marty and Scott Appleby, 116.
4. Loc. cit.
5. W. Dinges, 'Roman Catholic traditionalism in the United States,' in Marty and Scott Appleby, 89.
6. Dinges, art. cit., 97-8.
7. Ibid., 82.

CHAPTER TEN

1. A. P. d'Entrèves, *Natural law: an introduction to legal philosophy*, London, Hutchinson, 1951.
2. The Hart-Devlin debate started with reactions to the Wolfenden Report (on decriminalising homosexual acts), first with a lecture by Devlin (in 1959) at the British Academy, and then with two books, and some follow-up articles.
3. H. L. A. Hart, *Law, liberty and morality*, Oxford, Oxford University Press, 1963.
4. Patrick Devlin, *The Enforcement of morals*, Oxford, Oxford University Press, 1965.
5. Devlin, op. cit., 25.
6. John Courtney Murray, *We hold these truths: Catholic reflections on the American proposition*, New York, Sheed and Ward, 1960, 164.
7. Austin Flannery OP, ed., 'Pastoral constitution on the church in the modern world', *Vatican II: constitutions, decrees, declarations*, Dublin, Dominican Publications, 1996, 163-282.
8. Ladislas Örsy, 'Are church investigation procedures really just?' *Doctrine & Life*, Dublin, Dominican Publications, vol 48, n 8, October 1998, 453-66.
9. William T. Cavanaugh, *Theopolitical imagination: Christian practices of space and time*, Edinburgh, T&T Clarke, 2002.
10. Jean-Paul Marthoz and Joseph Saunders, 'Religion and the human rights movement', *World report 2005: events of 2004*, New York, Human Rights Watch, 2005, 40-69.

CHAPTER ELEVEN

1. John Henry Newman, *An Essay on the development of Christian doctrine*, (1845 edition) Middlesex, Penguin, 1974, 76.
2. Seán Fagan, *Does morality change?* Dublin, Columba Press, 2003, 192.
3. John Henry Newman, 'Letter to the Duke of Norfolk,' *Certain difficulties felt by Anglicans on Catholic teaching*, Vol II, London, 1891, Longman, Green & Co, 250.
4. Alan Donagan, *The Theory of morality*, Chicago, Chicago University Press, 1977, 142.

CHAPTER THIRTEEN

1. R. M. Doerflinger, 'The ethics of funding embryonic stem cell research: a Catholic viewpoint', *Kennedy Institute of Ethics Journal 9*, 1999, 137-150.
2. S. Holm, 'Going to the roots of the stem cell controversy', *Bioethics* 16, 2002, 497.
3. J. Harris, 'From the guest editor', *Bioethics* 16, 2002, ii-iv.
4. K. R. Chien, 'Lost in translation' *Nature* 428, 2004, 607-8.
5. C.A. Tauer, 'International policy failures: cloning and stem cell research', *Lancet*, 344, 209.

6. L. Cahill, 'Genetics, commodification, and social justice in the globalization era', *Kennedy Institute of Ethics Journal* 11, 2001, 221-238.
7. S. Holm, op. cit., 500-501.
8. R. Green, 'Benefiting from evil', *Bioethics* 16, 2002, 547. See also Howard Curser, 'The Ethics of embryonic stem cell research', *Journal of Medicine and Philosophy* 29, 2004, 533-562 and Julie Clague, 'Abortion and the use of foetal tissue in research and treatment: what is the connection', in *Ethics in crisis?* John Scally, ed., Veritas, 1997, 33-42.
9. R. Green, op. cit., 548-550.
10. Ibid., 555.
11. Ibid., 556.

The Contributors

Charles E. Curran, a priest of the diocese of Rochester, New York, is the Elizabeth Scurlock University Professor of Human Values at Southern Methodist University. He has served as president of three national academic societies in the United States. His latest book is *The Moral theology of Pope John Paul II*, (Washington, DC: Georgetown University Press, 2005).

Gabriel Daly is a member of the Order of St Augustine. He has been a lecturer in systematic and historical theology at Trinity College Dublin for many years and is an Honorary Fellow of the college. A former chairman of the Irish Theological Association, he has published widely. His books include *Transcendence and immanence: a study in Catholic modernism and integralism*, (Oxford: Clarendon Press, 1980) and *Creation and redemption*, (Dublin: Gill and Macmillan, 1988).

Seán Fagan, a Marist priest in Dublin, has more than forty years' experience teaching, counselling and writing in Europe, America, Africa, and Asia. He is the author of *Has sin changed?* and *Does morality change?* and more than one hundred articles on theology, spirituality and the religious life. He was Secretary General of the Society of Mary in Rome from 1983-1996.

Amelia Fleming is a graduate of the Pontifical University, Maynooth and lectures in theology in the Humanities Department in Carlow College. Her current research centres mainly on contemporary moral discourse in Irish society.

Raphael Gallagher is an Irish born Redemptorist. An Arts graduate of UCG, he did post-graduate theological studies in Italy and Germany. Apart from a period of administration work in his religious congregation he has been a Professor of Moral Theology in a number of universities. Currently he is an Invited Professor at the Alphonsian Academy in Rome.

Michael Glazier was born in Kerry. He has worked in America as an editor and publisher for over forty-five years. He most recently edited *The Encyclopedia of the Irish in America,* co-edited *The Encyclopedia of American Catholic history,* and in 2004 he edited the new edition of *The Modern Catholic encyclopedia.*

Angela Hanley is a co-ordinator in the Priory Institute distance education programme in theology. She is a contributor to religious periodicals and author of *Justified by faith: an Irish missionary experience in Malawi.* She is married to Gearoid O Brien and they are parents to an adult daughter and son.

Wilfrid John Harrington is an Irish Dominican priest. He studied theology in Rome and biblical studies at the École Biblique in Jerusalem. He is professor of scripture at the Dominican House of Studies, Dublin, senior lecturer at the Milltown Institute of Theology and visiting lecturer at the University of Dublin. He has taught summer courses in the United States regularly since 1965.

C. Denis Kelly is a science graduate of University College Dublin. His post-graduate studies were in Columbia University, New York, at McGill University, Montreal and Harvard Marketing. His professional career involved product and corporate marketing, post-corporate mergers restructuring and the re-organisation and development of industry at the national level, in preparation for Ireland's joining the European Common Market. He is married, has four children and thirteen grandchildren. All live in Dublin.

Justine McCarthy is the chief features writer and a columnist with *The Irish Independent* and a regular contributor to radio and television programmes. She wrote an unauthorised biography of the Irish President, entitled *Mary McAleese: The Outsider,* published by Blackwater Press.

John Scally is a native of Co Roscommon. He is Beresford Lecturer in Ecclesiastical History in the School of Religion and Theology in Trinity College, Dublin. His books include: *Whose death is it anyway?: euthanasia and the right to die; After the brave new world?: ethics and genetics* and *Doctor's orders?: towards a new medical ethics.*

David Smith is a member of the Missionaries of the Sacred Heart. He is also Visiting Senior Lecturer in Medical Ethics in the Royal College of Surgeons, Director of the MSc in Health Care Ethics and Law in RCSI and invited lecturer in Trinity College, University College Dublin, University College Cork and The Church of Ireland Theological College.

Anne Thurston studied theology as a mature student. She is the author of *Because of her testimony: the word in female experience,* (Gill & Macmillan 1995); *Knowing her place: gender and the gospels* (Gill & Macmillan 1998) and *A Time of waiting: images and insights,* (Columba Press 2004) and a regular contributor to religious journals. She is married with three grown-up children.

Bernard Treacy OP, is editor of *Doctrine & Life,* and director of Dominican Publications. A native of Roscommon, he has been a Dominican since 1963, and has been involved in the Order's publishing work since the mid-1970s.